I0023205

Joseph White

Better than pearls

Sacred songs expressly adapted for gospel meetings

Joseph White

Better than pearls
Sacred songs expressly adapted for gospel meetings

ISBN/EAN: 9783337264970

Printed in Europe, USA, Canada, Australia, Japan

Cover: Foto ©Thomas Meinert / pixelio.de

More available books at **www.hansebooks.com**

BETTER · THAN · PEARLS

SACRED SONGS

EXPRESSLY ADAPTED FOR

GOSPEL MEETINGS

BY

J. E. WHITE,

C. W. STONE,

A. B. OYEN,

BATTLE CREEK, MICH.:
PUBLISHED BY J. E. WHITE, 133 WEST MAIN STREET.

1881.

PREFACE.

—⚜—

BETTER THAN PEARLS contains only such pieces as by a careful examination of both words and music are found to be useful in all gospel meetings.

Thanks are tendered to those who have so liberally contributed to its pages treasures both new and old.

Hoping our efforts may help on the tide of sacred song here below, and that we may join with you in singing the great "new song" above,

We are respectfully yours,

J. E. WHITE.
C. W. STONE.
A. B. OYEN.

Copyrighted 1881, by J. E. WHITE.

Better than Pearls.

CROWN HIM LORD OF ALL.

J. E. WHITE.

1 All hail the pow'r of Je - sus' name! Let an - gels prostrate fall;
2 Sin-ners, whose love can ne'er for - get The worm-wood and the gall,
3 Oh, that with yon - der sac-red throng We at his feet may fall!

Bring forth the roy - al dia - a - dem, And crown him Lord of all.
Go, spread your trophies at his feet, And crown him Lord of all.
We'll join the ev - er - last - ing song, And crown him Lord of all.

DUET.

Ye cho - sen seed of Is-rael's race, Ye ransomed from the fall,
Let ev - 'ry kin - dred, ev - 'ry tribe, On this ter - res - trial ball,
Him Lord of lords, and King of kings, Let ev - 'ry na - tion call;

Hail him who saves you by his grace, And crown him, and crown him, and
To him all maj - es - ty as-cribe, And crown him, and crown him, and
From Heav'n to earth the chorus, rings, Yea, crown him, yea, crown him, yea,

(3)

Copyrighted 1881, by J. E. WHITE.

CROWN HIM LORD OF ALL.--Concluded.

crown him Lord of all. Hail him who saves you
crown him Lord of all. To him all maj-es-
crown him Lord of all. From Heav'n to earth the

by his grace, And crown him Lord of all.
ty as-cribe, And crown him Lord of all.
cho-rus rings, Yea, crown him Lord of all.

No. 2.

JESUS REIGNS.

W. O. PERKINS.

1 Je-sus rules and reigns a-bove, I shall see him by-and-by.
2 He is all in all to me, I shall see him by-and-by.
3 Just a lit-tle long-er here, I shall see him by-and-by.

In that realm of joy and love, I shall see him by-and-by,
With-out him what would I be? I shall see him by-and-by;
Then his bless-ed pres-ence near, I shall see him by-and-by.

(4)

By permission.

JESUS REIGNS.--Concluded.

As the ransom'd one of them, I may touch his garment's hem;
He is still my hope and choice, How I long to hear his voice,
In that gold-en day of days, I my fee-ble voice will raise;

The small notes may be sung or omitted.

Crown'd with roy-al di-a dem, I shall see him by-and-by.
Mid the ran-som'd to re-joice; I shall see him by-and-by.
Ev-er-more his song of praise; I shall see him by-and-by.

CHORUS.

I shall see him by-and by,

See him by-and-by, See him by and by,

In that land of joy and love, Where Je-sus reigns a

Where Je-sus, Je-sus

bove, I shall see him by and by.

reigns a bove.

(5)

BEAUTIFUL VALLEY OF EDEN.

REV. W. O. CUSHING.   WM. F. SHERWIN.

1 Beau - ti - ful val - ley of E - den! Sweet is thy noon - tide calm;
2 O - ver the heart of the mourn-er Shin - eth thy gold - en day,
3 There is the home of my Saviour; There, with the blood-wash'd throng,

O - ver the hearts of the wea - ry, Breathing thy waves of balm.
Wafting the songs of the an - gels Down from the far a - way.
O - ver the high-lands of glo - ry Roll - eth the great new song.

REFRAIN.

Beau - ti - ful val - ley of E-den, Home of the pure and blest, How

The pure and blest,

Rit........ ....

oft - en a - mid the wild bil - lows I dream of thy rest—sweet rest!

(6)   By permission.

NO. 4. NEARER THEE.

F. E. BELDEN.

FRANK M. DAVIS.

1 Near-er Thee and ev-er near-er, O thou con-stant, might-y
2 Thou canst save us and de-liv-er When the ev-il hosts as-
3 We accept of thy sal-va-tion, And like Thee would per-fect
4 With thy grace di-vine up-hold us Lest we sink be-neath the

Friend! Thou to me art more, and dear-er Than all
sail; Thou of mer-cies art the giv-er, Through Thy
be; O de-liv-er from temp-ta-tion—Draw us
wave; In Thy might-y arms en-fold us When we

joys that earth can lend. Near-er Thee,........ Near-er
prom-ise we pre-vail. Near-er Thee,
near-er, near-er Thee.
near the si-lent grave.

CHORUS.

Thee,..... Clos-er, clos-er to Thy side! In thy

Near-er Thee

keep-ing safe are we, With us ev-er-more a-bide.

Copyrighted 1881, by J. E. WHITE.

(7)

TRIUMPH BY-AND-BY.

DR. C. R. BLACKALL.   H. R. PALMER.

1 The prize is set be-fore us, To win, His words im-plore us,
2 We'll fol-low where he lead-eth, We'll pas-ture where he feed-eth,
3 Our home is bright a-bove us, No tri-als dark to move us,

The eye of God is o'er us, From on high, from on high;
We'll yield to him who plead-eth, From on high, from on high;
But Je-sus, dear, to love us, There on high, There on high;

His love-ing tones are call-ing, While sin is dark, ap-pall-ing;
Then naught from him shall sev-er, Our hope shall bright-en ev-er,
We'll give him best en-deav-or, And praise his name for-ev-er;

'Tis Je-sus gent-ly call-ing, He is nigh, He is nigh.
And faith shall fail us nev-er, He is nigh, He is nigh.
His ran-somed ones will nev-er, Nev-er die, Nev-er die.

CHORUS.

By-and-by we shall meet him, By-and-by we shall greet him,

(8)   By permission.

TRIUMPH BY-AND-BY.--Concluded.

And with Je - sus reign in glo - ry, By - and - by, By - and - by;

By - and - by we shall meet him, By - and - by we shall greet him,

And with Je - sus reign in glo - ry by - and - by.

No. 6.   I COME TO JESUS.   J. E. WHITE.

1 I lay my sins on Je - sus, The spot - less Lamb of God;
2 I lay my wants on Je - sus, All full-ness dwells in him;
3 I lay my griefs on Je - sus, My bur-dens and my cares;
4 I long to be like Je - sus, Meek, lov-ing, low - ly, mild:

He bears them all, and frees us From the ac - curs - ed load.
He heal - eth my dis - eas - es, He doth my soul re - deem.
He from them all re - leas - es, He all my sor - row shares.
I long to be like Je - sus, The Fa - ther's ho - ly child.

Copyrighted 1878, by J. E. WHITE.

(9)

No. 7. FATHER, WE COME TO THEE.

F. F. BELDEN.

W. J. BOSTWICK.

1 Fa - ther, we come to thee; No oth - er help have we; Thou wilt our
2 Save from our ma - ny foes, Save from our earth - ly woes; Be thou our
3 Give us thy grace di - vine, Seal us for - ev - er thine; Our way-ward

ref - uge be; On thee we call. Earth is but dark and drear
souls' re - pose In time of need. Doubt-ing are we, and weak;
feet in - cline From sin to flee. O guide us, we im - plore,

With-out thy pres - ence near; Be thou our com - fort here, Fath - er of all.
To us sweet cour-age speak; Thy mighty arm we seek For strength indeed.
'Till wea-ry life is o'er, And on a bright - er shore, We dwell with thee.

CHORUS.

Fa - ther, we come to thee, Turn not a - way;

Help - less we come to thee; Hear while we pray.

Copyrighted 1880, by J. E. WHITE.

No. 8. THE ROCK THAT IS HIGHER.

E. JOHNSON. W. G. FISCHER.

1 Oh, sometimes the shadows are deep, And rough seems the path to the goal,
2 Oh, sometimes how long seems the day, And sometimes how heavy my feet;
3 Oh, near to the Rock let me keep, Or blessings, or sorrows pre - vail;

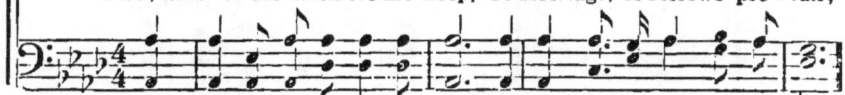

And sor-rows, how oft - en they sweep Like tempests down o-ver the soul.
But toil - ing in life's dust - y way, The Rock's blessed shadow, how sweet!
Or climb-ing the moun-tain way steep, Or walking the shad - ow - y vale.

CHORUS.

Oh, then to the Rock let me fly, let me fly, To the

Rock that is high - er than I: Oh, then to the
is high - er than I,

Rock let me fly, let me fly, To the rock that is high - er than I.

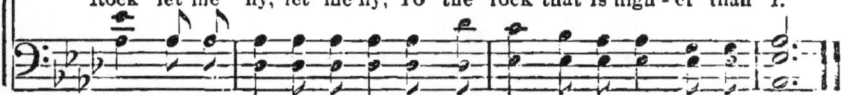

By permission. (11)

No. 9. On Jordan's Stormy Banks.

REV. SAMUEL STENNETT.

1 On   Jor-dan's storm·y banks I stand, And cast
2 O'er   all those wide - ex·tend·ed plains Shines one
3 When shall I reach that hap py place, And be f
4 Filled with de-light, my rap-tured soul Would here

To   Ca-naan's fair and hap py land, Where my p
There God the Son for - ev   er reigns, And scat-te
When shall I see my Fath-er's face, And in Hi
Tho' Jor-dan's waves a round me roll, Fearless I

CHORUS.

We will rest in the fair and hap - py land,
by ·

cross on the ev - er-green shore, . . . Sing the son
ev er green shore,

Lamb, by and by, And dwell with Je sus

By permission.

No. 10.   CROSS AND CROWN.

F. E. BELDEN.   D. S. HAKES.

1 There's a cross to be borne And a crown to be worn By
2 'Though the heart be op-press'd And we long for sweet rest—By
3 Ev - 'ry robe will be white, And the star - ry crowns bright, Which

some one, and who shall it be? 'Though the path-way be strait
life's heav - y bur-dens borne down— To the cross we will cling,
all of the ransomed shall wear; And the cit - y of gold

And our tri - als be great, The Sav - iour says, "Come, follow me."
For our tri - als shall bring A glo-rious ex-change for the crown.
Shall its port - als un - fold To us, if the cross here we bear.

CHORUS.

The cross........ and crown, ... The cross .... for the crown, ...

The cross and crown, the cross and crown, The crown for a cross, and the cross for a crown,

The cross we must bear if the crown we would wear, And Je - sus will wel-come us home.

By permission.   (13)

No. 11. He will Gather the Wheat in His Garner.

HARRIET B. M'KEEVER.　　　　　　　　　　　　　JNO. R. SWEENEY.

1 When Je · sus shall gath-er the na-tions Be-fore him at last to ap-
2 Shall we hear, from the lips of the Saviour, The words, Faithful servant, well
3 He will smile when he looks on his children, And sees on the ransomed his
4 Then let us be watch-ing and waiting,— Our lamps burning steady and
5 Thus liv - ing with hearts fixed on heaven, In pa - tience we wait for the

pear, Then, oh, how shall we stand in the judg - ment, When
done; Or, tremb - ling with fear and with an - guish, Be
seal; He will clothe them in Heav - en - ly beau-ty, As
bright,— When the Bride-groom shall call to the wedding Our
time, When, the days of our pil - grim - age end-ed, We'll

CHORUS.

summoned our sen - tence to hear? He will gath - er the wheat in his
banished a - way from his throne.
low at his foot-stool they kneel.
spir - its made read - y for flight.
back in the pres-ence di - vine.

gar - ner, But the chaff will he scat - ter a - way; Then, oh,

how shall we stand in the judg-ment Of the great Res - ur - rec - tion Day?

(14)

By permission.

No. 12. BLESSED ARE THEY THAT DO.

P. P. B.

P. P. BLISS.

Not too Slow.

1 Hear the words our Sav-iour hath spo-ken, Words of life un-
2 All in vain we hear his com-mand-ments, All in vain his
3 They with joy may en-ter the cit-y, Free from sin from

fail-ing and true; Careless one, prayerless one, hear and re-mem-ber,
prom-is-es too; Hear-ing them, fear-ing them, nev-er can save us,
sorrow and strife, Sanc-ti-fied, glo-ri-fied, now and for-ev-er,

CHORUS.

Je-sus says, "Blessed are they that do." Bless-ed are they that
Blessed, oh, bless-ed are they that do.
They may have right to the tree of life.

do his com-mand-ments, Blessed are they, bless-ed are they,

Blessed are they that do his commandments, Blessed, blessed, blessed are they.

By permission of JOHN CHURCH & CO

(15)

ONE DAY NEARER.

C. W. STONE.

1 O'er the hill the sun is set-ting, And the eve is drawing on,
2 One day near-er, sings the sail-or, As he glides the wa-ters o'er,
3 Worn and wea-ry, oft the pil-grim Hails the set-ting of the sun;
4 Nearer home! yes, one day near-er To our Fa-ther's house on high,

Slow-ly drops the gen-tle twi-light, For an-oth-er day is gone;
While the light is soft-ly dy-ing On his dis-tant na-tive shore.
For the goal is one day near-er, And his jour-ney near-ly done.
To the green fields and the fountains Of the land be-yond the sky.

Gone for aye, its race is o-ver, Soon the dark-er shades will come;
Thus the Chris-tian, on life's o-cean, As his light boat cuts the foam,
Thus we feel, when o'er life's des-ert Heart and san-dal worn we roam,
For the heav'ns grow bright-er o'er us, And the lamps hang in the dome,

Still 'tis sweet to know at ev-en, We are one day near-er home.
In the eve-ning cries with rap-ture, I am one day near-er home.
As the twi-light gath-ers o'er us, We are one day near-er home.
And our tents are pitched still clo-ser, For we're one day near-er home.

CHORUS.

Nearer home, (Near-er home,) Nearer home, (Near-er home,) Nearer

Copyrighted 1881, by C. W. STONE.

ONE DAY NEARER.—Concluded.

to our home on high, To the green fields and the
Near - er to our home on high, (on high,) green fields and the fountains,

foun - - - - tains Of the land be - yond the sky.
green fields and the fountains, Of the land be - yond the sky, Be - yond the sky.

No. 14.   **IN THE LIGHT.**

J. E. WHITE.

1 'Tis re - lig - ion that can give— In the light, in the light:
2 Je - sus will our ref - uge be— In the light, in the light:
3 Be the liv - ing God my Friend— In the light, in the light;
4 Then on Ca - naan's hap - py shore— In the light, in the light;

REFRAIN.

Sweet-est com-fort while we live—In the light of God. We will walk in the
'Till we shout the vic - to - ry In the light of God.
Then my bliss will nev - er end In the light of God.
We shall dwell for - ev - er-more In the light of God.

light, In the light, in the light, We will walk in the light, in the light of God.

Copyrighted 1881, by J. E. WHITE.

(17)

2

WE SHALL KNOW.

ANNIE HERBERT. J. H. ANDERSON.

1 When the mists have roll'd in splen-dor From the beau-ty of the hills,
2 If we err in hu-man blindness, And for-get that we are dust;
3 When the mists have risen above us, As our Fa-ther knows his own,

And the sun-shine, warm and ten-der, Falls in kiss-es on the rills,
If we miss the law of kind-ness When we strug-gle to be just,
Face to face with those that love us, We shall know as we are known,

We may read love's shin-ing let-ter In the rain-bow of the spray,
Snow-y wings of peace shall cov-er All the plain that hides a-way,—
Love, be-yond the o-rient meadows Floats the gold-en fringe of day,

We shall know each oth-er bet-ter When the mists have cleared a-way.
When the wea-ry watch is o-ver, And the mists have cleared a-way.
Heart to heart, we bide the shad-ows, Till the mists have cleared a-way.

By permission of S. BRANAIRD'S SONS.

WE SHALL KNOW.--Concluded.

CHORUS.

We shall know........ as we are known,... .... Nev-er-

We shall know   as we are known,

more............ to walk a - lone,   In the

Nev - er - more   to walk a - lone,

dawn - - - - ing of the morning, When the mists ..... have cleared a-

In the dawning of the morn-ing,   When the mists have cleared a-

way;   In the dawn - ing of the morn-ing,

way, have cleared a - way;   In the dawn-ing of the morning,

Rit......................

When the mists.............. have cleared a - way, have cleared a - way.

When the mists

(19)

F. E. BELDEN.
D. S. HAKES.

1 Sav - iour, Sav - iour, be my guide, For the way is dark and drear!
2 I am way-ward, I am weak, Oft - en falls the bit - ter tear;
3 Keep me, Sav-iour of my soul, Day by day, through ev'ry year;

Keep me ev - er near thy side, I am pressed by doubt and fear.
To my soul sweet comfort speak, As my help - er, Lord, ap - pear.
Self I yield to thy con - trol: In my heart thy stand - ard rear.

Sor-rows deep, and ills be - tide: Oh, my faint pe - ti - tion hear!
Make me pure, and make me strong, And thy pre - cepts to re - vere;
Oh, im - part thy peace di - vine! To my prayer now lend thine ear;

Come, and in my heart a - bide! Oh, for - ev - er be thou near!
Fill my heart with joy and song, Give my spir - it hope and cheer.
Own me as a child of thine: Keep me, keep me, Sav - iour dear!

CHORUS.

Keep me in the nar - - - row way,

Copyrighted 1880, by J. E. WHITE.

Keep me in the nar - row way,

Guide me, guide me ev - - 'ry day! Let me nev - er,

Guide me, guide me ev - 'ry day!

nev - - er stray! Keep me, Bless - ed One, I pray.

Let me nev - er, nev - er stray! Keep me, Bless - ed One, I pray.

No. 17. WORTHY IS THE LAMB.

1 Wor-thy, wor-thy is the Lamb, Wor-thy, wor-thy is the Lamb, Wor-thy, wor-thy
2 Sav-iour, let thy king-dom come! Now the man of sin consume—Bring thy blest mil-
3 Thus may we each mo-ment feel, Love him, serve him, praise him still, Till we all on

CHORUS.

is the Lamb That was slain. Glo - ry, hal - lo - lu - jah,
len - ni - um, Ho - - ly Lamb.
Zi-on's hill See the Lamb.

Praise him, hal - lo - lu - jah, Glo - ry, hal - lo - lu - jah to the Lamb.

No. 18. CLINGING AND RESTING.

REV. L. B. CARPENTER. JNO. R. SWENEY.

1 To the cross I long was cling-ing As a ref-uge from de-spair,—
2 To that cross I *cling* no long-er, Doubts and fears no lon-ger feel;
3 Oh, what needless griefs I've carried! And what needless burdens borne,
4 My sal-va-tion is com-plet-ed, Christ my hope, my life, my light;

Found re-lief from guilt of sin-ning While I lin-gered, cling-ing there:
Faith, and hope, and love are stronger, Je-sus' blood doth ful-ly heal.
All be-cause I, cling-ing, tar-ried, While the rest-ing was un-known.
Sin, and death, and hell de-feat-ed, Can-not now my soul af-fright.

Still life's waves and storms assailed me, Doubts and fears my mind distres't,
Now my song is not, "I'm clinging," That to me would now be loss,
Years of cling-ing were not wast-ed, Tho' they seem to me but loss,
Heav-en seems in bless-ed nearness, And earth's treasures are as dross,

And with all the cross a-vail'd me, Clinging gave no per-fect rest.
When mind, heart, and soul are sing-ing,—"I am *rest-ing* at the cross.
Since di-vin-er sweets I've tast-ed In this rest-ing at the cross.
While, 'mid light of cloud-less clearness, I am rest-ing at the cross.

CHORUS.

I was cling-ing, now I'm rest-ing, Sweetly rest-ing at the cross,

(22)

By permission.

CLINGING AND RESTING.--Concluded.

I was cling-ing, now I'm rest-ing, Sweetly rest-ing at the cross.

No. 19. STRIVING TO ENTER IN.

EDEN R. LATTA. FRANK M. DAVIS.

1 Striv-ing to fol-low Je-sus, E-ven as he hath said;
2 Striv-ing to fol-low Je-sus, E-ven thro' good and ill;
3 Striv-ing to fol-low Je-sus, E-ven with will-ing feet;
4 Striv-ing to fol-low Je-sus, Fol-low him to the end;

Keep-ing the nar-row path-way; Go-ing where he hath led!
Heed-ing his prec-ious coun-sels, Do-ing his ho-ly will.
Feel-ing his bless-ed guid-ance, Hear-ing his voice so sweet.
He will ac-cept and crown us; He is our constant friend.

CHORUS.

Striv-ing, striv-ing, Striv-ing a crown to win;
Striv-ing, striv-ing a crown to win,

Striv-ing, striv-ing, striv-ing to en-ter in.
Striv-ing, striv-ing a crown to win.

By permission.

(23)

CHRIST RETURNETH.

H. L. TURNER.

JAMES McGRANAHAN.

1 It may be at morn, when the day is a-wak-ing,
2 It may be at mid-day, it may be at twi light,
3 While its hosts cry, Ho-san-na, from Heav-en des-cend-ing,
4 Oh, joy! oh, de-light! should we go with-out dy-ing,

When sun-light thro' dark-ness and shad-ow is break-ing,
It may be per-chance, that the black-ness of mid-night
With glo-ri-fied saints and the an-gels at-tend-ing,
No sick-ness, no sad-ness, no dread, and no cry-ing,

That Je-sus will come in the full-ness of glo-ry,
Will burst in-to light in the blaze of his glo-ry,
With grace on his brow, like a ha-lo of glo-ry,
Caught up thro' the clouds with our Lord in-to glo-ry,

CHORUS.

To re-ceive from the world "His own." O Lord Je-sus, how
When Je-sus re-ceives "His own."
Will Je-sus re-ceive "His own."
When Je-sus re-ceives "His own."

long, how long Ere we shout the glad song, Christ re-turn-eth, Hal-le-

By permission of JOHN CHURCH & CO.

Rit......................

In - jah! hal - le - lu - jah! A - men, Hal - le - lu jah! A - men.

No. 21.

SHALL I LET HIM IN?

H. R. P.

H. R. PALMER.

Not too fast.

1 Christ is knock-ing at my sad heart; Shall I let him in?
2 Shall I send him the lov ing word? Shall I let him in?
3 Yes, I'll o - pen this proud heart's door? Yes, I'll let him in?

Pa tient ly plead-ing with my sad heart, Oh, shall I let him in?
Meek-ly ac - cept-ing my gra-cious Lord, Oh, shall I let him in?
Glad-ly I'll wel-come him ev - er - more; Oh, yes, I'll let him in.

Cold and proud is my heart with sin, Dark and cheer-less is all with - in;
He can in - fi - nite love im - part; He can par - don this reb-el heart;
Bless - ed Sav - iour, a-bide with me, Cares and tri - als will light-er be;

Christ is bid - ding me turn un - to him, Oh, shall I let him in?
Shall I bid him for - ev - er de part, Or, shall I let him in?
I am safe if I'm on - ly with thee, Oh, bless-ed Lord, come in.

By permission.

(25)

No. 22. HOME AND HEAVEN.

REV. J D. HAMMOND.

D. S. HAKES.

1 When mid toil and strife I wan-der, Far from
2 There I see its ra-diant brightness Far out
3 Let the thought of home and Heav-en, Help me,

When mid toil, &c.

home and those I love Faith points out my home up
shin ing light of sun; There I see the pearl-y
Lord, to do my best; Help me strug-gle as 'tis

Far from home, &c., I love, Faith points out, &c,

yon - der, God's own home of light and love.
white - ness, Of the robes through bat-tle won.
giv en, Till thou call me home to rest.

God's own home, &c.

REFRAIN.

Home and Heav'n, Home and Heav'n; Hap-py

Home and Heav'n, Home and Heav'n;

place so bright and fair, Home and Heav'n Home and

Happy place, so bright and fair, Home and Heav'n,

(26) Copyrighted 1879, by J. E. WHITE.

HOME AND HEAVEN.—Concluded.

Heav'n, Help me, Lord, to meet thee there.

to meet thee there.

Home and Heav'n, Help me, Lord, to meet thee there.

No. 23.

WE WOULD SEE HIM.

A. T. WORDON.

H. D. CLARKE.

1 We would see the Man of sor-rows, As he trod his toilsome way;
2 We would seek his smile and blessing, We would clasp that lov-ing hand;
3 We would see our Sav-iour dy-ing, That his chil-dren might go free,
4 We would see him rise tri-umphant, Burst the shackles of the grave;
5 We would see him come in splen-dor, When the earth shall pass a-way:

We would fol-low glad-ly with him, As he taught from day to day.
Sav-iour, help us, grop-ing blind-ly through a dark and lone-ly land.
Pray ing all the claims of Jus tice, With his blood up-on the tree.
Wel-comed by the au gel cho-rus, Might-y in his power to save.
Com ing in the clouds of heav-en, Ope' the gates of end-less day.

CHORUS.

We would see him, we would see him, Lov-ing Sav-iour of man-kind;

Might-y heal-er, stoop to hear us; We are poor, and weak, and blind.

Copyrighted 1879, by J. E. WHITE.

"I that saw thy soul's distress, A ransom gave;
"I the wine-press trod alone, 'Neath dark'ning skies;
I the bloody fight have won, Conquered the grave,

I that speak in righteousness, Might-y to save."
Of the people there was none Might-y to save."
Now the year of joy has come,— Might-y to save."

REFRAIN.

Might-y to save,....   Might-y to save,....
Might-y to save,   Might-y to save,

(28)   By permission.

No 25.   CLEANSING FOUNTAIN.   WESTERN MELODY.

1 There is a fountain filled with blood Drawn from Im-man-uels veins,
2 E'er since by faith, I saw the stream Thy flow-ing wounds sup-ply,
3 And in a no-bler, sweet-er song, I'll sing thy power to save,
4 Dear, dy-ing Lamb, thy pre-cious blood Shall nev-er loose its power,

Re-deem-ing love has been my theme, And shall be till I die,
And sin-ners plunged be-neath that flood Lose all their guil-ty stains,
When this poor, lisp-ing, stam'ring tongue Is ransomed from the grave,
Till all the ransomed church of God Be saved to sin no more.

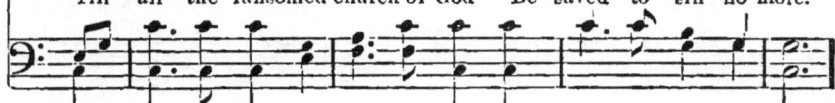

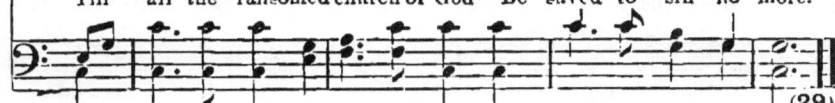

And shall be till I die, And shall be till I die,
Lose all their guil-ty stains. Lose all their guil-ty stains,
Is ran-somed from the grave. Is ran-somed from the grave,
Be saved to sin no more, Be saved to sin no more.

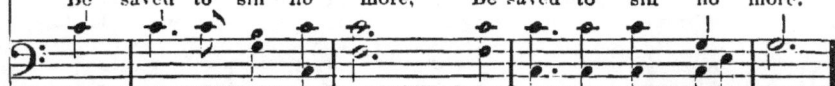

And sin-ners plunged beneath that flood Loose all their guil-ty stains.
Re-deem-ing love has been my theme, And shall be till I die.
When this poor, lisp-ing, stam'ring tongue Is ransomed from the grave.
Till all the ransomed church of God Be saved to sin no more.

(29)

No. 26. IS MY NAME WRITTEN THERE?

M A K

FRANK M. DAVIS.

1 Lord, I care not for rich-es, Nei-ther sil-ver nor gold;
2 Lord, my sins they are man y, Like the sands of the sea,
3 Oh! that beau-ti-ful cit-y, With its man-sions of light,

I would make sure of Heav-en, I would en-ter the fold;
But thy blood, O my Sav-iour, Is suf-fi-cient for me.
With its glo-ri-fied be-ings, In pure gar-ments of white;

In the book of thy king-dom, With its pag-es so fair,
For thy prom-ise is writ-ten In bright let-ters that glow,
Where no e-vil thing com-eth, To de-spoil what is fair;

Tell me, Je-sus, my Sav-iour, Is my name writ-ten there?
"Tho' your sins be as scar-let, I will make them like snow."
Where the an-gels are watch-ing,—Is my name writ-ten there?

CHORUS.

Is my name writ-ten there, On the page white and fair,

(30)

By permission.

IS MY NAME WRITTEN THERE?--Concluded.

In the book of thy king-dom, Is my name writ-ten there?

No. 27.   WHAT A FRIEND WE HAVE IN JESUS.

C. C. CONVERSE

1 What a friend we have in Je - sus,   All our sins and griefs to bear ;
2 Have we tri als and tempt - a tions?   Is there troub - le anywhere?
3 Are we weak and heav-y lad en, Cumbered with a load of care?

What a priv - i lege to car ry Ev - 'ry - thing to God in prayer!
We should nev-er be dis - cour-aged, Take it to the Lord in prayer.
Pre-cious Sav-iour, still our ref - uge! Take it to the Lord in prayer.

Oh! what peace we oft en for - feit,   Oh! what need-less pain we bear,
Can we find a friend so faith - ful, Who will all our sor-rows share?
Do thy friends des-pise, for-sake thee? Take it to the Lord in prayer;

All be-cause we do not car - ry   Ev - 'ry thing to God in prayer.
Je - sus knows our ev - ery weak-ness— Take it to the Lord in prayer.
In his arms he'll take and shield thee, Thou will find a sol-ace there.

By permission.   (31)

No. 28.   JESUS COME AND BLESS US.

E. R. LATTA.   W. O. PERKINS.

1 Jesus, thou hast promised, That when two or three In thy name have
2 Je-sus, thou hast met us Oft in sea-sons past; But we need thy
3 Je-sus, tune our voi-ces To the songs of praise; Be in each pe-

gath - ered, Thou wilt pres - ent be; And thy word be - liev - ing,
pres ence, With us till the last; Come, O bless - ed Sav - iour,
ti - tion, That to thee we raise; Let our faith grow stron - ger,

Now in prayer we kneel; Je-sus, come and bless us; Lord, thy self re - veal;
And thy grace dis - play; Hear us and ac - cept us; Bless us while we pray;
And our hope more bright; Let our love be pur - er, And our path more light;

CHORUS.

Je - sus, come and bless us, While we lin - ger here;

Je - sus, come and bless us; Be thou ev - er near.

(32)   By permission.

No. 29.

COME, THOU FOUNT.

Soprano Obligato.

J. E. WHITE.

1 Come, thou Fount of ev - 'ry bless ing, Tune my
2 Teach me some me - lo - dious son - net, Sung by

3 Je - sus sought me when a stran - ger, Wan - d'ring
4 Oh, to grace, how great a debt - or, Dai - ly

heart to sing thy grace; Streams of mer - cy
flam - ing tongues a bove; Praise the mount— I'm

from the fold of God; He, to res - cue
I'm con - strained to be; Let thy good - ness,

nev - er ceas - ing, Call for songs of loud - est praise.
fixed up - on it! Mount of thy re - deem - ing love.

me from dan - ger, In - ter - posed his pre - cious blood,
like a fet - ter Bind my wan - d'ring heart to thee.

Copyrighted 1881, by J. E. WHITE.

(33)

3

No. 30. WHEN WE LAY OUR BURDENS DOWN.

E. R. LATTA.   DR. W. O. PERKINS.

1 Tho' in life the tem-pests gath-er, And the clouds in black-ness frown,
2 Tho' the waves may rage a - bout - us, And the winds our voic-es drown,
3 When we sink be-neath our troub-les, And our hearts have weary grown,

We may hope for peace and qui - et, When we lay our bur-dens down!
Peace shall be up - on the wa - ters When we lay our bur-dens down!
Oh! how sweet to think of rest-ing, When we lay our bur-dens down!

We shall know no fear of dan - ger, And no doubts shall e'er as - sail,
We shall cast tri-umph - ant an-chor, In the home-land of the soul,
How it helps us on our jour - ney, To the bright for - ev - er more!

When our pil-grim-age is o - ver, And we pass be - yond the vail!
We shall reign with Him for-ev - er, Where the bil - lows nev-er roll!
To the man-sions o - ver yon-der, On the bright, ce - les - tial shore!

CHORUS.

We shall see him in his glo - ry, We shall wear a star-ry crown,

(34)   By permission.

WHEN WE LAY OUR BURDENS DOWN.—Concluded.

When we pass the shin - ing por - tals, When we lay our bur-dens down!

No. 31.   LOOK TO JESUS.

ELIZA H. MORTON.   ENGLISH MELODY.

1 Lift up the bowed head and re - joice in the Lord, Sing songs rich and
2 Ye wea - ry, oh, find in your Sav - iour sweet rest; By work - ing for
3 Then la - bor at morn - ing and la - bor at night, Thrust in the sharp
4 Oh, look to the glo - ry, the harp and the crown, Oh, look to the
5 Oh, think of the cit - y all gold - en and fair, Oh, think of the
6 Re - mem-ber, all beau - ty, all peace, and all love, Will blos - som in

CHORUS.

full, and de - light in thy God. Look to Je - sus, work for Je - sus; lo!
Je - sus your souls will be blest.
sick - le, the fields now are white.
life be - yond earth - ly re - nown.
robes that the ran-somed will wear.
bright - ness in bow - ers a - bove,

he is thy King! Look to Je - sus, work for Je - sus, his prais - es now sing!

(35)

No. 32. ONLY THEE.

CORIE F. DAVIS.

DR. W. O. PERKINS.

1 Have I need of aught, O Sav-iour, Aught on earth but thee?
2 Though I have of friends so man-y, Love, and gold, and health,
3 Who, like thee, can sooth and cheer me When in grief and tears?
4 Is there heart so kind and pa-tient With my fail-ings all?
5 Not for worlds would I ex-change it— This sweet faith in thee!
6 All my heart in this life need-eth, Find I, Lord in thee;

Have I an-y in the Heav-ens, An-y one but thee?
If I have not thee, my Sav-iour, Hold I an-y wealth?
Who, like thee, can sooth my pas-sions, Qui-et all my fears?
Or a voice more true and read-y, An-swer-ing my call?
Earth-ly treas-ures could not e-qual All thou are to me!
All my heart in Heav-en ask-eth Is, my Sav-iour, thee!

CHORUS.

On-ly thee, On-ly thee! Oh, the love the bliss shown me.
On-ly thee, on-ly thee!

On-ly thee, on-ly thee! None on earth but thee.
On-ly thee, on-ly thee!

Copyrighted 1881, by J. E. WHITE.

No. 33. THE CHRISTIAN.

E. A. BARNES.   C. W. STONE.

1 In the strife with sin and er - ror, Go-ing on in man-y
2 In this world of man - y bless - ings Blended oft with happy
3 From the care, the toil, the sor - row, That to all will surely

hearts, Who shall win, if not the Chris - tian, By the
days, Who has joy, if not the Chris - tian, Shun - ning
come, Who shall rest, if not the Chris - tian, In the

grace that God im - parts? In the Rock, the "Rock of
all for - bid - den ways? When the hand of stern af -
Fa - ther's bless - ed home? To the per - fect life in

A - ges," Seen by faith, and ev - er near, Who can
flic - tion O - ver - takes the strick-en one, Who can
Heav - en, When the storms of life are o'er, Who will

trust, if not the Christian, When the storms of life ap - pear?
say, if not the Christian, "Father, let thy will be done"?
come, if not the Christian, When this transient life is o'er?

Copyrighted 1881, by C. W. STONE.

No. 34.

H. K.

STAND UP FOR JESUS.

D. S. HAKES.

1 This life is a bat - tle 'gainst Sa - tan and sin,
2 To God for our ar - mor we'll fail not to go,
3 Sal - va - tion our hel - met, the Bi - ble our sword,
4 Tho' lit - tle temp - ta - tions— the worst ones of all—

And we are the sol - diers the vic t'ry to win, And
He'll clothe us with truth and with right - eous ness too; The
Though wi - ly our foes, we are strong in the Lord. While
Will of - ten be - set us to make us to fall, We'll

Christ is the cap - tain of our lit - tle band; What - ev - er op - pos - es, for
"gos - pel of peace" shall our footsteps attend, The good shield of faith from all
watching and praying our armor keeps bright. Our Je sus will help us to
stand up for Je - sus, and when life is o'er, For us he'll be stand - ing on

CHORUS.

him we will stand. Then stand up for Je - sus, Stand up for Je - sus,
harm shall defend.
stand for the right.
Jordan's bright shore.

Then stand for Je - sus, Stand for Je - sus,

Stand up for Je - sus, what-ev - er be - fall; Stand up for Je - sus,

Stand for Je - sus,

Copyrighted 1879, by J. E. WHITE.

STAND UP FOR JESUS.—Concluded.

Stand up for Je - sus, Oh, stand up for Je - sus, He stood for us all.

Stand for Je - sus,

No. 35.

LOVING KINDNESS.

MEDLEY.

1 A - wake, my soul, in joy - ful lays, And sing thy great Redeemer's praise;
2 He saw me ru - ined by the fall, Yet loved me, not - with-stand-ing all;
3 Tho' numerous hosts of might - y foes, Tho' earth and hell my way oppose,
4 I oft - en feel my sin - ful heart Prone from my Sav - iour to de - part;
5 Soon shall I pass the gloomy vale; Soon all my mor-tal powers must fail;

He just - ly claims a song from me. His lov - ing kind - ness, oh, how free!
He saved me from my lost es - tate: His lov - ing kind - ness, oh, how great!
He safe - ly leads my soul a - long, His lov - ing kind - ness, oh, how strong!
But though I oft have him for - got, His lov - ing kind - ness changes not.
Oh, may my last ex - pir - ing breath, His lov - ing kind - ness, sing in death.

His lov - ing kind - ness, lov-ing kind - ness, His lov - ing kind-ness, oh, how free!

(39)

No. 36.

TRAVELING TO ZION.

I. WATTS.

J. E. WHITE.

1 Come, ye that love the Lord, And let your joys be known,
2 Let those re-fuse to sing Who nev-er knew our God;
3 The hill of Zi-on yields A thousand sa-cred sweets,
4 Then let our songs a-bound, And ev-'ry tear be dry;

Join in a song with sweet ac-cord, And thus sur-round the throne.
But children of the heav'n-ly King, May speak their joys a-broad.
Be-fore we reach the heav'nly fields, Or walk the gold-en streets.
We're marching thro' Immanuel's ground, To fair-er worlds on high.

CHORUS.

We are trav - - 'ling to Zi - on,

We are trav - el - ing home-ward to Zi - ion,

Beau - ti - ful, beau - ti - ful Zi - on, We are

go-ing home to the cit-y of God, The saints' se-cure a - bode.

(40)

Copyrighted 1881, by J. E. WHITE.

No. 37. LISTEN, SAVIOUR.

THWING.

A. B. OYEN.

1 Sav-iour, blessed Sav-iour, Lis-ten whilst we sing,
2 Near-er, ev-er near-er, Christ, we draw to thee,
3 Great and ev-er great-er Are thy mer-cies here,

Hearts and voic-es rais-ing Prais-es to our King.
Deep in ad-o-ra-tion Bend-ing low the knee;
True and ev-er-last-ing Are the glo-ries there,

All we have we off-er, All we hope to be,
Thou for our re-demp-tion Cam'st on earth to die;
Where no pain or sorrow, Toil, or care, is known,

Bod-y, soul, and spir-it, All we yield to thee,
Thou, that we might fol-low, Hast gone up on high.
Where the an-gel-leg-ions Cir-cle round thy throne.

Copyrighted 1881, by J. E. WHITE.

(41)

No. 38.   BETTER THAN GOLD.

F. E. BELDEN.   L. O. EMERSON.

1 There are rich - es *bet - ter than gold,* Whose worth is ev - er the same,
2 There are rich - es *bet - ter than gold,* Than precious pearls of the sea,
3 There are rich - es *bet - ter than gold,* Which all the need - y may share,

There are price-less treas-ures un - told, That bear E - ter - ni-ty's name;
There is wealth your arms may en - fold—The cross of Christ may it be;
When the love of Christ they be - hold, And feel his ten - der - est care.

There are gems of truth to a-dorn the youth, Whose lus-tre nev-er shall fade;
For the cross is light if the heart is right, And al - ways read-y to bear,
In the ho - ly strife for the bet-ter life He aids the fearless and bold,

And they brightly shine from the word divine, In Heav-en's glo - ry ar-rayed.
And the crown is bright as the stars of night; But who is will-ing to wear?
For the righteous Lord hath a sure re-ward, And *Heav'n is bet-ter than gold.*

Cres.

And they brightly shine from the word divine, In Heav-en's glo-ry ar-rayed.
And the crown is bright as the stars of night; But who is will-ing to wear?
For the righteous Lord hath a sure reward, And *Heav'n is bet-ter than gold.*

(42)

Copyrighted 1881, by J. E. WHITE.

BETTER THAN GOLD.--Concluded.

CHORUS. Cres........................

Oh, the rich - es bet-ter than gold Are rich-es treas-ured on high;

They are peace and love, and a home a-bove, Where joys can nev-er die.

No. 39. JESUS CHRIST IS PASSING BY.

J. DENHAM SMITH.   MRS. JOS. F. KNAPP.

1 Je - sus Christ is pass - ing by, Sin - ner, lift to him thine eye;
2 Lo! he stands and calls to thee, "What wilt thou then have of me?"
3 "Lord, I would thy mer - cy see; Lord, re - veal thy love to me;
4 Oh, how sweet the touch of power Comes,—and is sal - va - tion's hour;

Rit.

As the pre - cious mo - ments flee. Cry, Be mer - ci - ful to me!
Rise, and tell him all thy need; Rise, he call - eth thee in-deed.
Let it pen - e - trate my soul, All my heart and life control."
Je - sus gives from guilt re - lease, "Faith hath saved thee, go in peace!"

By permission. (43)

1 We may sleep, but not for-ev-er, There will be a glorious dawn;
2 When we see a precious blos-som, That we tend-ed with such care,
3 We may sleep but not for-ev-er, In the lone and si-lent grave;

We shall meet to part, no, nev-er, On the res-ur-rec-tion morn.
Rudely ta-ken from our bosom, How our ach-ing hearts despair.
Blessed be the Lord that tak-eth, Blessed be the Lord that gave.

From the deep-est caves of o-cean From the des-ert and the plain,
Round the si-lent grave we lin-ger, Till the set-ting sun is low,
In the bright e-ter-nal cit-y Death can nev-er, nev-er come;

From the val-ley and the moun-tain, Countless throngs shall rise a-gain.
Feel-ing all our hopes have perish'd With the flow'r we cherished so.
In his own good time he'll call us From our rest to home, sweet home.

CHORUS.

We may sleep, but not for-ev-er, There will be a glorious dawn;

We shall meet to part, no, nev - er On the res - ur - rec-tion morn.

No. 41. LEAD THEM TO THEE.

Slowly.

FRANK M DAVIS.

1 Lead them, my God, to thee, Lead them to thee, These chil dren
2 When earth looks bright and fair, Fes - tive and gay, Let no de
3 E'en for such lit tle ones, Christ came a child, And thro' this
4 Yea though my faith be dim, I would be lieve, That thou this

dear of mine, Thou gav est me, Oh, by thy love di - vine,
lu - sive snare Lure them a stray; But from temp - ta tions pow'r,
world of sin Mov'd un - de filed; Oh, for his sake, I pray,
precious gift Wilt now re - ceive, Oh, take their young hearts now,

Lead them, my God, to thee, Lead them, lead them, lead them to thee.
Lead them, my God, to thee, Lead them, lead them, lead them to thee.
Lead them, my God, to thee, Lead them, lead them, lead them to thee.
Lead them, my God, to thee, Lead them, lead them, lead them to thee.

By permission.

(45)

No. 42. WHAT HAST THOU DONE FOR ME.

MISS F. R. HAVERGAL.

J. E. WHITE.

1 I gave my life for thee, My pre-cious blood I shed,
2 My Fa-ther's house of light,— My glo-ry-cir-cled throne
3 I suf-fered much for thee, More than thy tongue can tell,

That thou might'st ransomed be, And quickened from the dead;
I left for earth-ly night, For wand'rings sad and lone;
Of bitter-est ag-on-y, To res-cue thee from hell;

I gave, I gave my life for thee, What hast thou given for me?
I left, I left it all for thee, Hast thou left aught for me?
I've borne, I've borne it all for thee, What hast thou borne for me?

I gave, I gave my life for thee, What hast thou given for me?
I left, I left it all for thee, Hast thou left aught for me?
I've borne, I've borne it all for thee, What hast thou borne for me?

(46)

Copyrighted 1881, by J. E. WHITE.

THE CLEANSING WAVE.

MRS. PHŒBE PALMER.   MRS. JOS. F. KNAPP.

1 Oh, now I see the crim-son wave, The foun-tain deep and wide;
2 I see the new cre - a - tion rise, I hear the speaking blood;
3 I rise to walk in Heaven's own light, A-bove the world and sin;
4 A - maz - ing grace! 'tis Heaven below, To feel the blood ap-plied;

Je - sus, my Lord, might-y to save, Points to his wound-ed side.
It speaks! pol - lut - ed na - ture dies! Sinks 'neath the cleansing flood.
With heart made pure and garments white, And Christ en-thron'd with - in.
And Je - sus, on - ly Je - sus, know, My Je - sus cru - ci - fied.

CHORUS.

The cleansing stream, I see, I see! I plunge, and oh, it cleanseth me!

Oh, praise the Lord, It cleanseth me! It cleanseth me, yes, cleanseth me!

By permission.   (47)

No. 44. BLESSED BE HE THAT COMETH.

FROM THE GERMAN.

Sing ho-san-na! Blessed be he that com-eth in the name of the Lord! Ho-san-na in the high-est! He that cometh in the name of the Lord, He that cometh in the name of the Lord, Ho-san-na, ho-san-na, ho-san-na in the high-est, Ho san-na in the high-est. Be hon-or, do-min-ion, and power, and glo-ry ev-er in the high-est.

DUET.

No. 45. KEEP US NEAR THEE.

LAURA C. NOURSE.

DR. W. O. PERKINS.

1 Keep us near thee, O our Father! Teach our weary souls to
2 Keep us near thee, O our Father! Hold us close when sorrows
3 Keep us near thee, O our Father! Strengthen for the daily
4 Keep us near thee, O our Father! Nearer as the years roll

rest In the safe and qui - et keep - ing Of the
come; Till our trem - bling lips shall fal - ter, "Not my
strife; Let our thoughts and hearts up - ris - ing Seek a
on; Till at last 'mid loud ho - san - nas An - gels

CHORUS.

one who loves us best. Keep us near thee, O our
will, but thine, be done."
high - er, pur - er life.
shout the wel - come home. Keep us near

Fa - ther! Help us, Lord, to love and fear thee; Lead us
Help us, Lord

in thy way for - ev - er, Keep us, Fa - ther, near to thee.

Copyrighted 1881, by J. E. WHITE. (49)

4

No. 46. THEY SHALL SHINE AS THE SUN.

W. T. G.

W. T. GIFFE.

1 Cheer up, wea-ry heart, with joy may you run The
2 Stand firm, faint-ing heart, be brave in the right; The
3 Oh, prom-ise of God, it rings in my ear Like

race that be-fore you ap-pears; Of the right-cous 'tis said they shall
hel-met of faith you should wear; By the sword of his word and the
mu-sic I can-not de-scribe. I may shine as the sun if I

shine as the sun In the realms of e-ter-nal years.
power of his might, God will help you the cross to bear.
on-ly draw near To the Lamb who on Cal-v'ry died.

CHORUS.

They shall shine.................... as the sun................,

They shall shine as the sun, When their work is done, All

They shall shine... ....

they who their mas-ter o-bey, They shall shine as the sun,

(50)

Copyrighted 1881, by J. E. WHITE.

THEY SHALL SHINE AS THE SUN.—Concluded.

as the sun...........

When their work is done, With Je - sus through end - less day.

No. 47.   JESUS IS MINE.

MRS. BONAR.   J. E. WHITE.

1 Fade, fade, each earthly joy; Je - sus is mine; Break ev - 'ry
2 Tempt not my soul a - way; Je - sus is mine; Here would I
3 Farewell, ye dreams of night; Je - sus is mine; Lost in this
4 Farewell, mor - tal - i - ty; Je - sus is mine; Hail! im - mor-

ten - der tie; Je - sus is mine. Dark is the wil - der-ness;
ev - er stay; Je - sus is mine. Per - ish - ing things of clay,
dawning bright; Je - sus is mine. All that my soul has tried,
tal - i - ty; Je - sus is mine. Wel - come, O lov'd and blest;

Earth has no rest - ing-place; Je-sus a-lone can bless; Je - sus is mine.
Born but for one brief day, Pass from this earth away; Je - sus is mine.
Left but a dismal void, Je-sus has sat - is - fied; Je - sus is mine.
Welcome, sweet scenes of rest; Welcome, my Saviour's breast; Jesus is mine.

Copyrighted 1879, by J. E. WHITE.

GOOD NEWS.

JAMES McGRANAHAN.

1 Good news from Heav'n, good news for thee, There flows a par - don, full and free,
2 Good news from Heav'n, good news for thee, The Sav - iour cries, "Come un - to me
3 Good news from Heav'n, good news for thee, Has ech - oed from e - ter - ni - ty;

To guil - ty sin - ners, thro' the blood Of the In - car - nate Son of God;
All ye who toil, with fears op - prest; Come, wea - ry one, oh, come and rest:"
And loud shall our ho - san - nas ring, When with the ran - som'd throng we sing,

He paid the debt that thou didst owe, He suf - fered death for thee be - low,
He loves thee with o'er - flow - ing love, He hears thy pray'r in Heav'n a - bove;
"Wor - thy the Lamb," whose pre - cious blood Has made us kings and priests to God;

He bore the wrath di - vine for thee, He groan'd and bled on Cal - va - ry.
He all thy past - ure shall pre - pare, And lead thee with a shepherd's care.
Our harps we'll tune to nob - lest strains, And glo - ry give to him who reigns.

CHORUS.

Good news from Heav'n, good news for thee, There flows a par - don, full and free,

By permission of JOHN CHURCH & CO.

GOOD NEWS.—Concluded.

To guilt - y sin - ners thro' the blood Of the In - car - nate Son of God.

No. 49. JESUS IS PASSING.

F. E. BELDEN.   D. S. HAKES.

1 Je - sus is pass - ing, Je - sus is pass - ing; Come, all ye
2 Je - sus is pass - ing, Je - sus is pass - ing; Come now, ye
3 Je - sus is pass - ing, Je - sus is pass - ing; Come, all ye
4 Je - sus is pass - ing, Je - sus is pass - ing: Come, ye af -

blind, and re - ceive now your sight. He will bend o'er thee,
lame, to the Heal - er of all. His arm can shield thee,
poor, to the plen - te - ous store. Now he will lead thee,
flict - ed by sin and by shame. Oh, we im - plore thee,

He will re - store thee; He will ex - change all thy dark - ness for
One look can heal thee: He will at - tend to the poor cripple's
Ev - er will feed thee; Je - sus in - vites thee to hun - ger no
Let him re - store thee; Come while he lin - gers and call eth thy

light; Come, and thy Sav - iour will give thee thy sight.
call; Now he is pass - ing, is pass - ing for all.
more; Come to the boun - ti - ful heav - en - ly store.
name; Come, all ye la - den with sin and with shame.

Copyrighted 1878, by J. E. WHITE.

(53)

GO AND INQUIRE.

W. A. O.

W. A. OGDEN.

1 Searching the Scrip-tures, the bless-ed Scriptures,
2 Searching the Scrip-tures, the bless-ed Scriptures,
3 Searching the Scrip-tures, the bless-ed Scriptures,

Seek - ing the Sav - iour day by day, Striv - ing to
Seek - ing to know the heav'n - ly way, Try - ing to
Seek - ing the wan - d'rers by the way, Try - ing to

learn the wondrous sto - ry, What does the bless - ed Bi - ble say?
reach the gold - en cit - y, What does the bless - ed Bi - ble say?
point a soul to Je - sus, What does the bless - ed Bi - ble say?

CHORUS.

Go and in-quire,............ the King command-eth, Ask of the

Go and in-quire, the King command - eth,

Lord............ for me and thee; Knock at the o - - - - pen door of

Ask of the Lord for me and thee; Knock at the o - pen door of

(54)

By permission.

mer - cy, Where there is par - - don full and free.

mer - cy, Where there is par - don full and free.

No. 51.　　THE SOLID ROCK.

EDWARD MOTE.　　　　　　　　　　　　　　J. E. WHITE.

1 My hope is built on noth - ing less Than Je - sus' blood and
2 When dark-ness veils his love - ly face, I rest on his un -
3 His oath, his cov - e - nant, his blood, Sup - port me in the
4 When he shall come with trum-pet sound, Oh, may I then in

right - eous - ness; I dare not trust the sweet - est frame, But
chang - ing grace; In ev - er - y high and storm - y gale, My
whelm - ing flood; When all a - round my soul gives way, He
him be found; Dress'd in his right - eous - ness a - lone, Fault-

CHORUS.

whol-ly lean on Je - sus' name. On Christ, the Sol - id Rock, I stand; All
an-chor holds within the vail.
then is all my hope and stay.
less to stand be-fore the throne!

oth - er ground is sink-ing sand, All oth - er ground is sink-ing sand.

Copyrighted 1881, by J. E. WHITE.

(55)

No. 52. I Love to Tell the Story.

MISS KATE HANKEY. W. G. FISCHER.

1 I love to tell the sto-ry Of un-seen things a-bove,
2 I love to tell the sto-ry! More won-der-ful it seems,
3 I love to tell the sto-ry! 'Tis pleas-ant to re-peat
4 I love to tell the sto-ry! For those who know it best

Of Je-sus and his glo-ry Of Je-sus and his love!
Than all the gold-en fan-cies Of all our gold-en dreams.
What seems, each time I tell it, More won-der-ful-ly sweet.
Seem hun-ger-ing and thirst-ing To hear it like the rest.

I love to tell the sto-ry! Be-cause I know it's true;
I love to tell the sto-ry! It did so much for me!
I love to tell the sto-ry; For some have nev-er heard
And when, in scenes of glo-ry, I sing the new, new song.

It sat-is-fies my long-ings, As noth-ing else would do.
And that is just the rea-son I tell it now to thee.
The mes-sage of sal-va-tion From God's own Ho-ly Word.
'Twill be—the old, old sto-ry That I have loved so long.

CHORUS.

I love to tell the sto-ry! 'Twill be my theme in Glo-ry,

(56)

By permission.

I Love to Tell the Story.—Concluded.

To tell the old, old sto ry Of Je-sus and his love.

No. 53.

W A. O.

When Thou Comest.

W. A. OGDEN.

1 When thou com - est in thy king-dom, Je-sus, Lord, re-mem-ber me,
2 When thou com - est in thy king-dom, Sin-ful tho' my heart may be,
3 When thou com - est in thy king-dom, Mounting upward to the skies,

Thus the pen-i-tent thief, en-treat - ed Christ the Lord, on Cal - va - ry.
Like the pen-i-tent thief, I pray thee, Je-sus, Lord, re-mem-ber me.
Like the pen-i-tent thief, I pray to Be with thee in Par-a-dise.

CHORUS.

Nev-er in vain Nev-er in vain, Faith in-spires this wonderful strain.

When thou com est in thy king-dom, Je - sus, Lord, re-mem-ber me.

By permission.

(57)

No. 54. **I AM COMING TO THE CROSS.**

REV. WM. McDONALD.   WM. G. FISCHER.

1 I am com - ing to the cross; I am poor, and weak, and blind;
2 Long my heart has sighed for thee, Long has e - vil reigned with - in;
3 Here I give my all to thee, Friends and time, and earth-ly store;
4 In thy prom - is - es I trust, Now I feel the blood ap - plied:

CHO.—I am trust - ing, Lord, in thee, O thou Lamb of Cal - va - ry;

I am count - ing all but dross, I shall full sal - va - tion find.
Je - sus sweet - ly speaks to me,— "I will cleanse you from all sin."
Soul and bod - y thine to be,— Whol - ly thine for - ev - er - more.
I am pros - trate in the dust, I with Christ am cru - ci - fied.

Hum - bly at thy cross I bow, Save me, Je - sus, save me, now.

By permission.

No. 55. **MY ALL TO THEE.**

HAVERGAL.   T. C. O'KANE.

1 I bring my sins to thee, The sins I can - not count, That
2 My heart to thee I bring, The heart I can - not read, A
3 To thee I bring my care, The care I can - not flee, Thou
4 I bring my grief to thee, The grief I can - not tell; No
5 My joys to thee I bring, The joys thy love has given, That
6 My life I bring to thee, I would not be my own; O

all may cleansed be, In the once opened fount. I bring them,
faithless, wand'ring thing, An e - vil heart in-deed. I bring it,
wilt not on - ly share, But take it all for me. O, lov - ing
words shall needed be, Thou knowest all so well, I bring the
each may be a wing To lift me near - er Heaven. I bring them,
Saviour, let me be Thine, ev - er thine a - lone. My heart, my

(58)   By permission.

My All to Thee.—Concluded.

Sav-iour, all to thee, The bur - den is too great for me.
Sav-iour, now to thee, That fixed and faith - ful it may be.
Sav-iour, now to thee, I bring the load that wearies me.
sor-row laid on me, O suff - 'ring Sav - iour! all to thee.
Sav-iour, all to thee, Who hast pro - cured them all for me.
life, my all, I bring To thee, my Sav - iour and my King.

No 56.   LIKE AS A FATHER.

F. E. BELDEN.   D. S. HAKES.

1 "Like as a fa - ther" pit - ies his child, So the Lord
2 "Like as a fa - ther" when we be - lieve, Mer - ci - ful
3 "Like as a fa - ther," ev - er the same, He that cre -
4 "Like as a fa - ther," con - stant is he, God in com -

pit - ies the sin - ner de - filed; Wait - eth in kind - ness,
still, he will glad - ly re - ceive; List - ens to hear us,
a - ted and know - eth our frame; Watch - eth the stray - ing,
pas - sion re - gard - eth our plea; In need he com - eth,

Pit - ies our blindness, Long-eth to welcome, though of - ten re - viled.
Bless - es to cheer us, Pit - ies when - ev - er his Spir - it we grieve.
Guardeth the pray - ing, Bids us to trust in his al - might - y name.
Pre-cious his promise, Fa - ther in Heaven for - ev - er to be.

Copyrighted 1878, by J. E. WHITE.   (59)

SAVIOUR LEAD US.

DOROTHY THRUPP.

Soprano Obligato.

J. E. WHITE.

1 Sav - iour, like a shepherd lead us, Much we need thy constant
2 We are thine, do thou befriend us, Be the Guard-ian of our

1 Sav-iour, like a shep-herd lead us, Much we need thy
2 We are thine, do thou be-friend us, Be the Guard - - ian

care; In thy pleas-ant pas-tures feed us,
way; Keep thy flock, from sin de - fend us,

con - stant care; In thy pleas - - ant pas-tures feed us,
of our way; Keep thy flock, from sin de - fend us,

For our use thy folds prepare.
Seek us when we go a - stray.

CHORUS.

For our need thy folds pre - pare. Bless - ed Je - sus! bless - ed
Seek us when wo go a - stray.

Copyrighted 1881, by J. E. WHITE.

SAVIOUR LEAD US.--Concluded.

Je - sus! Thou hast bought us, thine we are; Bless - ed

Je - sus! bless - ed Je - sus! Thou hast bought us, thine we are (we are).

WILL YOU MEET US?

No. 58.

SLAVE MELODY.

1 Say, broth - ers, will you meet us?   Say, broth - ers, will you meet us?
2 Say, sis - ters, will you meet us?   Say, sis - ters, will you meet us?
3 By the grace of God we'll meet you,   By the grace of God we'll meet you,
4 That will be a hap - py meet - ing,   That will be a hap - py meet-ing,
5 Jesus lives and reigns for - ev - er,   Jesus lives and reigns for - ev - er,

Say, broth - ers, . will you meet us On Ca - naan's hap - py shore?
Say, sis - ters, will you meet us On Ca - naan's hap - py shore?
By the grace of God we'll meet you, On Ca - naan's hap - py shore.
That will be a hap - py meet - ing On Ca - naan's hap - py shore.
Jesus lives and reigns for - ev - er On Ca - naan's hap - py shore.

HAKES.

F. E. B.

F. E. BELDEN.

1 There is sweet rest for feet now wea-ry, In the rugged, upward way;
2 For that blest morn our hearts are longing, When shall end earth's night of woe;
3 Soon to that cit-y, bright, e-ter-nal, Wea-ry pilgrims all shall go;
4 Fa-ther above, in mercy guide us To those mansions of the blest;

There is a morn when midnight dreary Shall be lost in per-fect day.
When, thro' those pearly portals thronging, Mor-tal cares we'll leave be-low.
Soon we shall rest in pastures ver-nal, Where life's waters cease-less flow.
Safe in the Rock of A-ges hide us 'Till we gain our fi-nal rest.

Copyrighted 1878, by J. E. WHITE.

No. 60.

BAPTIZE US ANEW.

W. A. O.

W. A. OGDEN.

Spirited.

1 Bap-tize us a-new With fire from on high, With love, oh, re-
2 Un-wor-thy, we cry, Un-ho-ly, un-clean, Oh, wash us, and
3 O heav-en-ly Dove, De-scend from on high, We plead thy rich
4 Oh, list the glad voice, From Heav-en it came, "Thou art my be-

CHORUS.

fresh us, Dear Sav-iour, draw nigh. We hum-bly be-seech thee, Lord
cleanse us, From sin's guilt-y stain.
bless-ing, In mer-cy draw nigh. *Last verse.*
lov-ed, Well pleas-ed I am." We praise thee, we bless thee, Dear

By permission.

BAPTIZE US ANEW.—Concluded.

Je - sus, we pray, With fire and the Spir-it Bap - tize us to - day.
Lamb that was slain, We laud and a - dore thee, A - men and A - men.

No. 61. ## THE DAY IS AT HAND.

D. S. HAKES.

1 O'er the dis - tant mountain breaking, Comes the red-'ning dawn of day;
2 O, thou long ex - pect - ed, wea - ry Waits my anx - ious soul for thee;
4 Near - er is my soul's sal - va - tion, Spent the night, the day at hand;

Rise, my soul, from sleep a - wak-ing, Rise and sing, and watch, and pray,
Life is dark and earth is drea - ry, Where thy light I do not see,
Keep me in my low - ly sta-tion, Watch-ing for thee, till I stand,

'Tis thy Sav - iour, 'Tis thy Sav-iour, On his bright re - turn-ing way.
O my Sav - iour, O my Sav-iour, When wilt thou re - turn to me?
O my Sav - iour, O my Sav-iour, In the bright and promised land.

Copyrighted 1879, by J. E. WHITE.

No. 62. BEULAH LAND.

EDGAR PAGE.　　　　　　　　　　　　　　　　　　　JNO. R. SWENEY.

1 I've reach'd the land of corn and wine, And all its rich-es free-ly mine,
2 The Saviour comes and walks with me, And sweet communion here have we,
3 A sweet perfume up-on the breeze Is borne from ev-er-ver-nal trees,
4 The zephyrs seem to float to me, Sweet sounds of Heaven's mel-o-dy,

Here shines undimm'd one bliss-ful day, For all my might has pass'd a-way.
He gent-ly leads me with his hand, For this is Heaven's bor-der land.
And flow'rs that never fad-ing grow Where streams of life for-ev-er flow.
As angels, with the white-robed throng, Join in the sweet redemption song.

CHORUS.

O Beu-lah land, sweet Beu-lah land, As on thy high-est mount I stand,

I look a-way a-cross the sea, Where mansions are prepared for me,

And view the shin-ing glo-ry shore, My Heav'n, my home for-ev-er-more.

(64)　　　　　　By permission.

No. 63. WONDROUS LOVE.

WM. G FISCHER

1 God loved the world of sin ners lost, And ruined by the fall;
2 Ev'n now by faith I claim him mine, The ris - en Son of God,
3 Love brings the glorious full - ness in, And to his saints makes known
4 Be - liev ing souls, re - joic - ing go; There shall to you be given
5 Of vic - tory now o'er Sa - tan's power Let all the ransomed sing,

Sal - va - tion full, at high - est cost, He of - fers free to all.
Re - demp-tion by his death I find, And cleansing thro' the blood.
The bless - ed rest from in - bred sin, Thro' faith in Christ a lone.
A glo - rious foretaste, here be low, Of end - less life in Heaven.
And tri - umph in the dy - ing hour Thro' Christ the Lord, our King.

CHORUS.

Oh, 'twas love, 'twas wondrous love! The love of God to me·

It brought my Sav - iour from a - bove, To die on Cal - va - ry.

By permission.

(65)

No. 64.

RUBLEE.

EBEN E. REXFORD.

JOSEPH GARRISON.

1 They brought their gifts to Je-sus, And laid them at his feet,
2 A - part from oth - er giv - ers, A poor way-far - er stood,
3 "Dear Lord," he cried in sor - row, "I know how kind thou art,·

And love for this dear Sav - iour, Made ev - 'ry off - 'ring sweet;
He saw the gifts they of - fered, The poor - est count - ed good.
Take all I have to give thee, My sin - ful, way - ward heart."

Good deeds and words of kind-ness, Help for the poor of earth,
And he was filled with long - ing, A gift, though poor, to bring;
Then Je - sus an - swered soft - ly, "Count not the gift as small,

And not a gift a - mong them, Was thought of lit - tle worth.
A - las! all emp - ty-hand - ed He stood be - fore the King.
· Tho' all of them are pre - cious, Thine is the best of all."

CHORUS.

Wouldst bring a gift to Je - sus That he will count most sweet?

(66)

From CHURCH AND PRAYER MEETING SONGS, by permission.

RUBLEE.—Concluded.

Say, "Lord, my heart I give thee," And lay it at his feet.

No. 65. **EDITH.**

E. M. C.

E. MANFORD CLARK.

Prayerfully.

1 No, not my power, but thine, O Lord! Can suc-cor me, or peace afford;
2 No, not my power, O Saviour dear, Can soothe one pain, can dry one tear;
3 No, not my power, most ho - ly One, Can comfort when life's race is run,
4 No, not my power, Almighty God, Could stand beneath thy chast'ning rod;
5 No, not my power, O Lord of earth, Can save me from the jaws of death;

Thy Spir - it, Lord, thy gen - tle voice A - lone can make this heart rejoice!
How soon would fail my fee - ble pow'r, Except thou help me ev - 'ry hour!
A - las! the help of man how vain, Except thy Spir - it, Lord, remain!
Ex - cept thou, Lord, in love ap - pear, To draw thy ho - ly Spir - it near!
'Tis thou, thy Spir - it, Lord, I need! 'Tis thou a-lone canst raise the dead!

CHORUS.

No, not my power—nor aught I have—Nor aught in earth can be my stay;

'Tis thou, and thou a - lone, canst save! O Lord, I need thee ev - 'ry day.

No. 66. SEEK AND FIND.

F. E. BELDEN.

FRANK M. DAVIS.

1. Bur - dened soul, there's rest in Je - sus; Seek and find, seek and find; From our
2. Would we share the Sav - iour's bless-ing? Seek and find, seek and find; Un - to
3. Would we dwell a - bove for - ev - er? Seek and find, seek and find; There are

ev - 'ry load he frees us—Great is his com - pas - sion kind; He who
all, their sins con - fess - ing, Will his mer - cy be in - clined. Are we
ties no hand can sev - er, That in love our hearts shall bind. Are we

car - eth for us all Will up - hold us lest we fall; For when - e'er we
weak and faint with fear? If we speak, he waits to hear; And his wondrous
wea - ry of the strife In this world with trouble rife? We may dwell where

CHORUS.

kneel, he sees us, And will an - swer when we call. Seek and find, seek and find,
love ex - press-ing, Will be - stow us strength and cheer.
sor - row nev - er Mars a glad, e - ter - nal life.

All ye la - den, weak and wea - ry, Seek and find, seek and find, Seek, and ye shall find.

Copyrighted 1881, by J. E. WHITE.

DUKE STREET. L. M.

J. HATTON.

67   Jehovah's Power.

1 Before Jehovah's awful throne,
  Ye nations, bow with sacred joy;
Know that the Lord is God alone;
  He can create, and he destroy.

2 His sovereign power, without our aid,
  Made us of clay, and formed us men;
And when, like wandering sheep we
    strayed,
  He brought us to his fold again.

3 We'll crowd thy gates with thankful
    songs,
High as the heavens our voices raise,
And earth, with her ten thousand tongues,
  Shall fill thy courts with sounding
    praise.

4 Wide as the world is thy command;
  Vast as eternity thy love ·
Firm as a rock thy truth shall stand,
  When rolling years shall cease to move.

68   Preach the Word.

1 Go, preach my gospel, saith the Lord;
  Bid the whole world my grace receive;
He shall be saved who trusts my word;
  And they condemned who disbelieve.

2 I'll make your great commission known,
  And ye shall prove my gospel true
By all the works that I have done,
  By all the wonders ye shall do.

3 Teach all the nations my commands;
  I'm with you till the world shall end;
All power is vested in my hands,
  I can destroy, and I defend.

4 He spake, and light shone round his
    head;
On a bright cloud to Heaven he rode;
They to the farthest nations spread
  The grace of their ascended Lord.

69   God's Goodness.

1 High in the heavens, Eternal God,
  Thy goodness in full glory shines,
Thy truth shall break through ev'ry cloud
  That veils thy just and wise designs

2 Forever firm thy justice stands,
  As mountains their foundations keep,
Wise as the wonders of thy hands,
  Thy judgments are a mighty deep

3 O God, how excellent thy grace,
  Whence all our hope and comfort
    spring!
The sons of Adam, in distress,
  Fly to the shadow of thy wing.

4 In the provisions of thy house
  We still shall find a sweet repast;
There mercy like a river flows,
  And brings salvation to our taste.

5 Life, like a fountain, rich and free,
  Springs from the presence of my Lord,
And in thy light our souls shall see
  The glories promised in thy word.

70   Star of Our Hope.

1 Star of our hope! he'll soon appear,
  The last loud trumpet speaks him near;
Hail him, all saints, from pole to pole—
  How welcome to the faithful soul!

2 From Heaven angelic voices sound.
  Behold the Lord of glory crowned,
Arrayed in majesty divine,
  And in his highest glories shine.

3 The grave yields up its precious trust,
  Which long has slumbered in the dust,
Resplendent forms ascending fair,
  To meet the Saviour in the air.

4 Descending with his azure throne,
  He claims the kingdom for his own;
The saints rejoice, they shout, they sing,
  And hail him their triumphant King

71   Father, Bless the Word.

1 Almighty Father, bless the word,
  Which, through thy grace, we now have
    heard,
Oh! may the precious seed take root,
  Spring up, and bear abundant fruit.

2 We praise thee for the means of grace,
  Thus in thy courts to seek thy face ·
Grant, Lord, that we who worship here,
  May all at length, in Heaven appear.

(69)

RETREAT. L. M.   DR. HASTINGS.

72   The Mercy Seat.

1 From every stormy wind that blows,
  From every swelling tide of woes,
  There is a calm, a sure retreat,
  'Tis found beneath the mercy-seat.

2 There is a scene where spirits blend,
  Where friend holds fellowship with
    friend;
  Though sundered far, by faith they meet
  Around one common mercy-seat?

3 Ah! whither should we flee for aid,
  When tempted, desolate, dismayed,
  Or how the hosts of hell defeat,
  Had suffering saints no mercy-seat?

4 There, there on angels' wings we soar,
  And sin and sense seem all no more;
  The Lord comes down, our souls to greet,
  And glory crowns the mercy-seat.

73   Earthly Trials.

1 One precious boon, O Lord, I seek,
  While tossed upon life's billowy sea;
  To hear a voice within me speak,
  Thy Saviour is well pleased with thee.
        [bear.

2 Earth's scoffs and scorn well pleased I'll
  Nor mourn though under foot I'm trod,
  If day by day I may but share
  Thine approbation, O my God.

3 Let me but know, where'er I roam,
  That I am doing Jesus' will; [home,
  And though I've neither friends nor
  My heart shall glow with gladness still.

4 To that bright, blest, immortal morn
  By holy prophets long foretold,
  My eager, longing eyes I turn,
  And soon its glories shall behold.

74   Invocation.

1 Thy presence, gracious Lord, afford;
  Prepare us to receive thy word;
  Now let thy voice engage our ear,
  And faith be mixed with what we hear.

2 To each thy sacred word apply
  With sovereign power and energy,
  And may we in thy faith and fear
  Reduce to practice what we hear

75   Life is Fleeting.

1 How vain is all beneath the skies!
  How transient every earthly bliss!
  How slender all the fondest ties
  That bind us to a world like this!

2 The evening cloud, the morning dew,
  The with'ring grass, the fading flower,
  Of earthly hopes are emblems true—
  The glory of a passing hour.

3 But though earth's fairest blossoms die,
  And all beneath the skies is vain,
  There is a land whose confines lie
  Beyond the reach of care and pain.

4 Then let the hope of joys to come
  Dispel our cares, and chase our fears:
  If God be ours, we're traveling home,
  Though passing through a vale of tears.

76   Christ Present.

1 Where two or three, with sweet accord,
  Obedient to their sovereign Lord,
  Meet to recount his acts of grace,
  And offer solemn prayer and praise,

2 There, says the Saviour, will I be,
  Amid this little company;
  To them unveil my smiling face,
  And shed my glories round the place.

3 We meet at thy command, dear Lord,
  Relying on thy faithful word;
  Now send thy Spirit from above,
  Now fill our hearts with heavenly love.

77   God's Love and Care.

1 My God, how endless is thy love!
  Thy gifts are every evening new,
  And morning mercies from above,
  Gently descend like early dew.

2 Thou spread'st the curtains of the night,
  Great Guardian of my sleeping hours;
  Thy sov'reign word restores the light
  And quickens all my drowsy powers.

3 I yield myself to thy command,
  To thee devote my nights and days;
  Perpetual blessings from thy hand,
  Demand perpetual songs of praise.

(70)

78   Commencing Sabbath.

1 Another six days' work is done,
Another Sabbath is begun:
Return, my soul, enjoy thy rest,
Improve the day that God has blest.

2 Come, bless the Lord, whose love assigns
So sweet a rest to weary minds:
A blessed antepast is given,
On this day more than all the seven.

3 Oh! that our tho'ts and thanks may rise
As grateful incense to the skies:
And draw from Christ that sweet repose
Which none but he who feels it knows.

4 This heavenly calm within the breast
Is the best pledge of glorious rest,
Which for the church of God remains,
The end of cares, the end of pains.

79   He Cares for Me.

1 Thus far the Lord has led me on;
Thus far his power prolongs my days:
And every evening shall make known
Some fresh memorial of his grace.

2 Much of my time has run to waste,
And I, perhaps, am near my home;
But he forgives my follies past, [come.
And gives me strength for days to

3 I lay my body down to sleep;
Peace is the pillow for my head;
While well-appointed angels keep
Their watchful stations round my bed.

4 Thus if the night of death should come,
My flesh shall rest beneath the ground,
And wait thy voice to break my tomb,
With sweet salvation in the sound

80   Come, Holy Spirit.

1 Come, Holy Spirit, heavenly guest,
And make thy mansion in my breast;
Dispel my doubts, my fears control,
And heal the anguish of my soul.

Thou God of love and peace divine,
Oh, make thy light within me shine!
Forgive my sins, my guilt remove,
And send the tokens of thy love.

81   Sabbath Prayer.

1 Lord of the Sabbath, hear us pray,
In this thy house, on this thy day;
Accept, as grateful sacrifice,
The songs which from thy temple rise.

2 Thine earthly Sabbaths, Lord, we love,
But there's a nobler rest above;
To that our laboring souls aspire,
With ardent hope and strong desire.

3 O long-expected day, begin,
Dawn on these realms of woe and sin;
Fain would I leave this weary road,
And go to meet my blessed Lord.

82   God's Counsel.

1 God, in the gospel of his Son,
Makes his eternal counsels known,
'Tis here his richest mercy shines,
And truth is drawn in fairest lines.

2 Wisdom its dictates here imparts,
To form our minds, to cheer our hearts;
Its influence makes the sinner live;
It bids the drooping saint revive.

3 Our raging passions it controls,
And comfort yields to contrite souls,
It brings a better word in view,
And guides us all our journey through,

83   Christ Our Pattern.

1 My blest Redeemer and my Lord,
I read my duty in thy word;
But in thy life the law appears,
Drawn out in living characters.

2 What truth and love thy bosom fill!
What zeal to do thy Father's will!
Such zeal, and truth, and love divine,
I would transcribe, and make them mine.

3 Cold mountains and the midnight air
Witnessed the fervor of thy prayer;
The desert thy temptations knew,
Thy conflict, and thy victory too.

4 Be thou my pattern: make me bear
More of thy gracious image here; [name
Then God, the Judge, shall own my
Among the followers of the Lamb,

(71)

McCABE. L. M.

84   Wondrous Cross.

1 When I survey the wondrous cross
  On which the Prince of glory died,
My richest gain I count but loss,
  And pour contempt on all my pride.

2 See, from his head, his hands, his feet,
  Sorrow and love flow mingled down;
Did e'er such love and sorrow meet?
  Or thorns compose so rich a crown?

3 Since I, who was undone and lost,
  Have pardon through his name and
    word;
Forbid it, then, that I should boast,
  Save in the cross of Christ, my Lord.

4 Were the whole realm of nature mine,
  That were a tribute far too small;
Love so amazing, so divine,
  Demands my life, my soul, my all.

WARREN. L. M.
V. C. TAYLOR.

85   Praise to God.

1 O thou, to whom, in ancient time,
  The psalmist's sacred harp was strong,
Whom kings adored in song sublime,
  And prophets praised with glowing
    tongue, —

2 Not now on Zion's hight alone
  Thy favored worshipers may dwell,
Nor where, at sultry noon, thy Son
  Sat weary by the patriarch's well.

3 From every place below the skies,
  The grateful song, the fervent prayer—
The incense of the heart—may rise
  To Heaven, and find acceptance there.

86   Praise Expressed.

1 So let our lips and lives express
  The holy gospel we profess;
So let our works and virtues shine,
  To prove the doctrine all divine.

2 Thus shall we best proclaim abroad
  The honors of our gracious Lord,
When his salvation reigns within,
  And grace subdues the power of sin.

3 Religion bears our spirits up,
  While we expect that blessed hope,
The bright appearing of the Lord;
  And faith stands leaning on his word.

MIGDOL. L. M.

DR. LOWELL MASON.

87 The Fountain.

1 By faith I to the fountain fly,
Opened for all mankind and me,
To purge my sins of deepest dye, —
My life and heart's impurity.

2 From Christ, the smitten rock, it flows,
The purple and the crystal stream;
Pardon and holiness bestows,
And both I gain through faith in him.

88 Sabbath Light.

1 Lord of the Sabbath and its light,
I hail thy hallowed day of rest;
It is my weary soul's delight,
The solace of my care-worn breast.

2 O sacred day of peace and joy,
Thy hours are ever dear to me;
Ne'er may a sinful thought destroy
The holy calm I find in thee.

3 How sweetly now they glide along!
How hallowed is the calm they yield!
Transporting is their rapturous song,
And heavenly visions seem revealed.

4 O Jesus, let me ever hail
Thy presence with the day of rest;
Then will thy servant never fail
To deem thy Sabbath doubly blest.

89 Ashamed of Jesus!

1 Jesus, and shall it ever be,
A mortal man ashamed of thee?
Ashamed of thee, whom angels praise,
Whose glories shine through endless days?

2 Ashamed of Jesus! that dear friend
On whom my hopes of Heaven depend!
No; when I blush, be this my shame,
That I no more revere his name.

3 Ashamed of Jesus! yes, I may,
When I've no guilt to wash away,
No tears to wipe, no good to crave,
No fears to quell, no soul to save.

4 Till then, nor is my boasting vain,
Till then, I boast a Saviour slain;
And oh! may this my glory be,
That Christ is not ashamed of me.

90 By Faith.

1 'Tis by the faith of joys to come,
We walk through deserts dark as night:
Till we arrive at Heaven, our home,
Truth is our guide, and faith our light.

2 The want of sight she well supplies;
She makes the pearly gates appear;
Far into distant worlds she pries,
And brings eternal glories near.

3 Though lions roar, and tempests blow,
And rocks and dangers fill the way,
With joy we tread the desert through,
While faith inspires a heavenly ray.

91 God's Work.

1 Sweet is the work, my God, my King,
To praise thy name, give thanks, and sing;
To show thy love by morning light,
And talk of all thy truth by night.

2 Sweet is the day of sacred rest:
No mortal cares shall seize my breast;
Oh! may my heart in tune be found,
Like David's harp of solemn sound.

3 When grace has purified my heart,
Then I shall share a glorious part;
And fresh supplies of joy be shed,
Like holy oil to cheer my head.

4 Then shall I see, and hear, and know,
All I desired or wished below;
And every hour find sweet employ,
In that eternal world of joy.

92 Plea for Grace.

1 Ere to the world again we go,
To meet its cares and idle show,
Thy grace, once more, O God, we crave,
From folly and from sin to save.

2 May the great truths we here have heard,
The lessons of thy holy word,
Dwell in our inmost bosoms deep,
And all our souls from error keep.

3 Oh! may the influence of this day
Long as our memory with us stay,
And as an angel guardian prove,
To guide us to our home above.

(73)

SESSIONS. L. M.　　　L. O. EMERSON.

93　Jesus Reigns.

1 He reigns! the Lord, the Saviour reigns!
Sing to his name in lofty strains;
Let all the saints in songs rejoice,
And in his praise exalt their voice.

2 Deep are his counsels, and unknown;
But grace and truth support his throne;
Though gloomy clouds his way surround,
Justice is their eternal ground.

3 In robes of judgment, lo, he comes!
Shakes the wide earth, and cleaves the
　　tombs;
Before him burns devouring fire;
The mountains melt, the seas retire.

4 His enemies with wild dismay
Fly from the sight, and shun the day;
Then lift your heads, ye saints, on high,
And sing, for your redemption's nigh.

94　Come, Gracious Spirit.

1 Come, gracious Spirit, heavenly Dove,
With light and comfort from above;
Be thou our guardian, thou our guide;
O'er all our thoughts and steps preside.

2 To us the light of truth display,
And make us know and choose thy way;
Plant holy fear in every heart,
That we from God may ne'er depart.

3 Lead us to holiness—the road
Which we must take to dwell with God;
Lead us to Christ—the living way,
Nor let us from his pastures stray;

4 Lead us to God—our final rest,—
To be with him forever blest;
Lead us to Heaven, its bliss to share—
Fullness of joy forever there.

95　The Sabbath.

1 I love thine earthly Sabbaths, Lord,
For they are days of holy rest, [word,
And thou hast passed thy changeless
That they shall be forever blest.

2 I love thine earthly Sabbaths, Lord,
That congregate thy people here,
To join their hearts in sweet accord,
And fit them for a higher sphere.

96　Grant Thy Blessing.

1 Lord, grant thy blessing here to-day;
Oh! give thy people joy and peace;
The tokens of thy love display,
And favor that shall never cease.

2 We seek the truth which Jesus brought;
His path of light we long to tread;
Here be his holy doctrines taught,
And here their purest influence shed.

3 May faith, and hope, and love, abound;
Our sins and errors be forgiven;
And we, from day to day, be found
Children of God and heirs of Heaven.

97　Dedication Hymn.

1 All things are thine: no gift have we,
Lord of all gifts! to offer thee;
And hence, with grateful hearts to-day,
Thine own, before thy feet we lay.

2 Thy will was in the builder's thought;
Thy hand unseen amidst us wrought;
Through mortal motive, scheme, and
Thy wise, eternal purpose, ran. [plan,

3 No lack thy perfect fullness knew;
For human needs and longings grew
This house of prayer, this home of rest—
Here may thy saints be often blest.

4 In weakness and in want we call
On thee, for whom the heavens are
Thy glory is thy children's good, [small;
Thy joy thy tender fatherhood.

5 O Father! deign these walls to bless;
Make this th' abode of righteousness!
And let these doors a gateway be
To lead us from ourselves to thee!

98　Closing Hymn.

1 Dismiss us with thy blessing, Lord,
Help us to feed upon thy word;
All that has been amiss, forgive,
And let thy truth within us live.

2 Though we are guilty, thou art good;
Cleanse us from sin through Jesus' blood;
Give every fettered soul release,
And bid us all depart in peace.

(74)

99   Compassion.

1 The God of love will sure indulge
  The flowing tear, the heaving sigh,
When death inflicts his fatal wound,
  When tender friends and kindred die.

2 Yet not one anxious, murm'ring thought
  Should with our mourning passions
    blend,
Nor would our bleeding hearts forget
  Th' alm'g'ty, ever-living Friend.

3 Beneath a num'rous train of ills,
  Our feeble flesh and heart may fail;
Yet shall our hope in thee, our God,
  O'er every gloomy fear prevail.

4 Our Father, God! to thee we look,
  Our rock, our portion, and our friend;
And on thy covenant love and truth,
  Our sinking souls shall still depend.

100   Just as I Am.

1 Just as I am—without one plea,
  But that thy blood was shed for me,
And that thou bid'st me come to thee,
  O Lamb of God, I come, I come.

2 Just as I am—and waiting not
  To rid my soul of one dark blot,
To thee, whose blood can cleanse each
  O Lamb of God, I come, I come. [spot.

3 Just as I am—though tossed about
  With many a conflict, many a doubt—
"Fightings within, and fears without,"
  O Lamb of God, I come, I come.

4 Just as I am—poor, wretched, blind—
  Sight, riches, healing of the mind,
Yea, all I need, in thee to find,
  O Lamb of God, I come, I come.

5 Just as I am—thou wilt receive,
  Wilt welcome, pardon, cleanse, relieve;
Because thy promise I believe,
  O Lamb of God, I come, I come.

6 Just as I am—thy love, I own,
  Has broken every barrier down;
Now to be thine, and thine alone,
  O Lamb of God, I come, I come.

101   Prayer.

1 What various hind'rances we meet,
  In coming to the mercy-seat;
Yet, who that knows the worth of
  But wishes to be often there. [prayer,

2 Prayer makes the darkest cloud with-
    draw;
Prayer climbs the ladder Jacob saw,
Gives exercise to faith and love,
Brings every blessing from above.

3 Restraining prayer, we cease to fight;
Prayer makes the Christian's armor
And Satan trembles when he sees [bright;
The weakest saint upon his knees.

4 When Moses stood with arms spread
  Success was found on Israel's side; [wide,
But when, through weariness, they
  That moment Amalek prevailed. [failed,

5 Have you no words? Ah! think again;
  Words flow apace when you complain,
And fill your fellow-creatures ears
  With the sad tale of all your cares.

6 Were half the breath thus vainly spent,
  To Heaven in supplication sent,
Your cheerful song would oftener be,
  Hear what the Lord hath done for me!

102   Asleep in Jesus.

1 Asleep in Jesus! Blessed sleep,
  From which none ever wake to weep;
A calm and undisturbed repose,
  Unbroken by the last of foes.

2 Asleep in Jesus! Oh, how sweet
  To be for such a slumber meet!
With holy confidence to rest
  In hope of being ever blest.

3 Asleep in Jesus! Peaceful rest,
  Whose waking is supremely blest;
No fear, no woe, shall dim that hour,
  That manifests the Saviour's power.

4 Asleep in Jesus! Soon to rise,
  When the last trump shall rend the skies;
Then burst the fetters of the tomb,
  To wake in full, immortal bloom.

OLDEN. L. M.

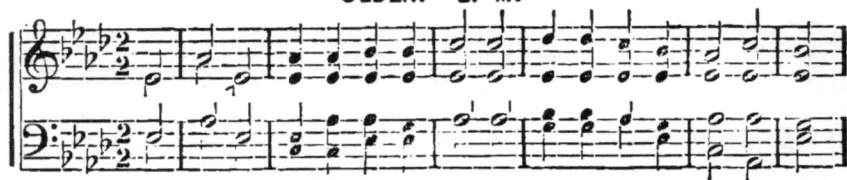

103   Christ's Prayer.

1 'Tis midnight—and on Olive's brow,
  The star is dimmed that lately shone;
  'Tis midnight—in the garden now
  The suffering Saviour prays alone.

2 'Tis midnight—and, from all removed,
  The Saviour wrestles lone with fears;
  E'en that disciple whom he loved
  Heeds not his Master's grief and tears.

3 'Tis midnight—and, for others' guilt,
  The man of sorrows weeps in blood;
  Yet he, who hath in anguish knelt,
  Is not forsaken by his God.

4 'Tis midnight—and, from ether plains,
  Is borne the song that angels know;
  Unheard by mortals are the strains
  That sweetly soothe the Saviour's woe.

104   Salvation.

1 Let everlasting glories crown
  Thy head, my Saviour and my Lord;
  Thy hands have brought salvation down,
  And stored the blessings in thy word.

2 In vain the trembling conscience seeks
  Some solid ground to rest upon:
  With deep distress the spirit breaks,
  Till we apply to Christ alone.

3 How well thy blessed truths agree!
  How wise and holy thy commands!
  Thy promises, how firm they be!
  How sure our hope and comfort stands!

4 Should all the forms that men devise
  Assault my faith with treach'rous art,
  I'd call them vanity and lies,
  And bind the gospel to my heart.

105   Prayer.

1 Prayer is appointed to convey
  The blessings God designs to give;
  Long as they live should Christians pray;
  They learn to pray when first they live.

2 If pains afflict, or wrongs oppress,
  If cares distract, or fears dismay,
  If guilt deject, if sin distress,
  In every case, still watch and pray.

(,6)

3 'Tis prayer supports the soul that's weak,
  Though thought be broken, language lame;
  Pray, if thou canst or canst not speak,
  But pray with faith, in Jesus' name

4 Depend on him; thou canst not fail;
  Make all thy wants and wishes known;
  Fear not, his merits must prevail!
  Ask but in faith, it shall be done.

106   The Maker's Love.

1 When power divine, in mortal form,
  Hushed with a word the raging storm,
  In soothing accents Jesus said,
  Lo, it is I; be not afraid.

2 So when in silence nature sleeps,
  And lonely watch the mourner keeps,
  One thought shall every pang remove,
  Trust, feeble man, thy Maker's love.

3 And when the last, dread hour shall come,
  While trembling nature waits her doom,
  This voice shall wake the righteous
  Lo, it is I, be not afraid.   [dead—

107   Dedication.

1 Here, in thy name, Eternal God,
  We build this earthly house for thee;
  Oh! choose it for thy fixed abode,
  And guard it long from error free.

2 When here, O Lord, we seek thy face,
  And dying sinners pray to live.
  Hear thou in Heaven, thy dwelling-place,
  And when thou hearest, Lord, forgive.

3 When here thy messengers proclaim
  The blessed gospel of thy Son,
  Still, by the power of his great name,
  Be mighty signs and wonders done.

4 And when our voices raise the song,
  Hosanna! to our heavenly King,
  Let Heaven with earth the strain prolong;
  Hosanna! let the angels sing.

108   Doxology.

Praise God from whom all blessings flow!
Praise him all creatures here below!
Praise him above, ye heavenly host!
Praise Father, Son, and Holy Ghost!

109   Trust in the Almighty.

1 Unshaken as the sacred hills,
    And firm as mountains stand,
Firm as a rock the soul shall rest
    That trusts th' Almighty hand.

2 Not walls nor hills could guard so well
    Fair Salem's happy ground,
As those eternal arms of love,
    That every saint surround.

110   The Word of God.

1 Father of mercies, in thy word
    What endless glory shines!
Forever be thy name adored
    For these celestial lines.

2 Here the Redeemer's welcome voice
    Spreads heavenly peace around;
And life and everlasting joys
    Attend the blissful sound.

3 Oh! may these heavenly pages be
    My ever dear delight;
And still new beauties may I see,
    And still increasing light.

111   The Saviour's Death.

1 Alas, and did my Saviour bleed?
    And did my Sovereign die?
Would he devote that sacred head
    For such a worm as I?

2 Was it for crimes that I have done
    He groaned upon the tree?
Amazing pity! grace unknown!
    And love beyond degree!

3 Well might the sun in darkness hide,
    And shut his glories in,
When Christ the Lord was crucified
    For man the creature's sin.

4 Thus might I hide my blushing face,
    While his dear cross appears,
Dissolve my heart in thankfulness,
    And melt mine eyes to tears.

5 But drops of grief can ne'er repay
    The debt of love I owe;
Here, Lord, I give myself away—
    'Tis all that I can do.

112   The Judgment.

1 And must I be to Judgment brought,
    And answer in that day,
For every vain and idle thought,
    And every word I say?

2 Yes; every secret of my heart
    Shall shortly be made known,
And I receive my just desert
    For all that I have done.

3 How careful, then, ought I to live!
    With what religious fear,
Who such a strict account must give
    For my behaviour here!

4 Thou awful Judge of quick and dead,
    The watchful power bestow;
So shall I to my ways take heed,
    To all I speak or do.

113   Accept Our Prayer.

1 Father! whate'er of earthly bliss
    Thy sovereign will denies,
Accepted at thy throne of grace,
    Let this petition rise:

2 Give me a calm, a thankful heart,
    From every murmur free;
The blessings of thy grace impart,
    And make me live to thee.

3 Let the sweet hope that thou art mine
    Through all my life attend,
Thy presence through my journey shine,
    And crown my journey's end.

114   The Book Divine.

1 How precious is the book divine,
    By inspiration given!
Bright as a lamp its doctrines shine,
    To guide our souls to Heaven.

2 It sweetly cheers our drooping hearts
    In this dark vale of tears,
And life, and light, and joy imparts,
    And banishes our fears.

3 This lamp, through all the tedious night
    Of life, shall guide our way,
Till we behold the clearer light
    Of an eternal day.

115   Awake, My Soul.

1 Awake, my soul! stretch every nerve,
  And press with vigor on;
A heavenly race demands thy zeal,
  And an immortal crown.

2 'Tis God's all-animating voice,
  That calls thee from on high;
'Tis he whose hand presents the prize
  To thine aspiring eye.

3 A cloud of witnesses around
  Hold thee in full survey;
Forget the steps already trod,
  And onward urge thy way.

4 Blest Saviour! introduced by thee,
  Our race have we begun:
And, crowned with vict'ry, at thy feet
  We'll lay our trophies down.

116   Blessed Bible.

1 There is an ancient, blessed book,
  Sent down from age to age;
Admiring angels bend to look
  Upon its hallowed page.

2 Preserved by wondrous care and skill,
  For our instruction given,
It speaks of God, and shows his will,
  And points the way to Heaven.

3 Oh! let us seek for heavenly grace
  To hear and read aright!
Till we behold the Saviour's face,
  And faith gives place to sight.

117   Salvation Nigh.

1 Awake, ye saints, and raise your eyes,
  And raise your voices high;
Awake, and praise that sovereign love
  That shows salvation nigh.

2 On all the wings of time it flies;
  Each moment brings it near:
Then welcome each declining day,
  Welcome each closing year.

3 Not many years their round shall run,
  Not many mornings rise,
Ere all its glories stand revealed
  To our admiring eyes.

(78)

118   Christian Soldier.

1 Am I a soldier of the cross,
  A follower of the Lamb?
And shall I fear to own his cause?
  Or blush to speak his name?

2 Must I be carried to the skies
  On flowery beds of ease,
Whilst others fought to win the prize,
  And sailed through bloody seas?

3 Are there no foes for me to face?
  Must I not stem the flood?
Is this vile world a friend of grace,
  To help me on to God?

4 Sure I must fight if I would reign;
  Increase my courage, Lord;
I'll bear the toil, endure the pain,
  Supported by thy word.

5 Thy saints in all this glorious war
  Shall conquer though they die;
They see the triumph from afar,
  With faith's discerning eye.

6 When that illustrious day shall rise,
  And all thy armies shine
In robes of vict'ry through the skies,
  The glory shall be thine.

119   Title Clear.

1 When I can read my title clear,
  To mansions in the skies,
I'll bid farewell to every fear,
  And wipe my weeping eyes.

2 Should earth against my soul engage,
  And fiery darts be hurled,
Then I can smile at Satan's rage,
  And face a frowning world.

3 Let cares like a wild deluge come,
  And storms of sorrow fall;
May I but safely reach my home,
  My God, my Heaven, my all.

4 There shall I bathe my weary soul
  In seas of heavenly rest,
And not a wave of trouble roll
  Across my peaceful breast.

BALERMA. C. M.

H. WILSON.

120   Plea for Faith.

1 Oh! for a faith that will not shrink,
   Though pressed by many a foe;
That will not tremble on the brink
   Of poverty or woe.

2 That will not murmur or complain
   Beneath the chastening rod;
But in the hour of grief or pain,
   Can lean upon its God.

3 A faith that shines more bright and clear
   When tempests rage without;
That when in danger knows no fear,
   In darkness feels no doubt;

4 That bears unmoved the world's dread
   Nor heeds its scornful smile; [frown,
That sin's wild ocean cannot drown,
   Nor its soft arts beguile.

5 Lord, give me such a faith as this,
   And then, whate'er may come,
I'll taste e'en here the hallowed bliss
   Of an eternal home.

121   A New Heart.

1 Oh, for a heart to praise my God!
   A heart from sin set free!
A heart that's sprinkled with the blood
   So freely shed for me!

2 A heart resigned, submissive, meek,
   My dear Redeemer's throne;
Where only Christ is heard to speak,
   Where Jesus reigns alone!

3 A humble, lowly, contrite heart,
   Believing, true, and clean,
Which neither life nor death can part
   From him that dwells within.

4 A heart in every thought renewed,
   And filled with love divine!
Perfect, and right, and pure, and good,
   A copy, Lord, of thine!

5 Thy nature, gracious Lord, impart;
   Come quickly from above;
Write thy new name upon my heart,
   Thy new, best name of love.

122   Closer to God.

1 Oh! for a closer walk with God,
   A calm and heavenly frame,
A light to shine upon the road
   That leads me to the Lamb.

2 Return, O holy Dove, return,
   Sweet messenger of rest;
I hate the sins that made thee mourn,
   And drove thee from my breast.

3 The dearest idol I have known,
   Whate'er that idol be,
Help me to tear it from thy throne,
   And worship only thee.

4 So shall my walk be close with God,
   Calm and serene my frame;
So purer light shall mark the road
   That leads me to the Lamb.

123   Redeemer's Praise.

1 Oh, for a thousand tongues, to sing
   My great Redeemer's praise!
The glories of my God and King,
   The triumphs of his grace.

2 Jesus, the name that calms our fears,
   That bids our sorrows cease!
'Tis music in the sinner's ears,
   'Tis life, and health, and peace.

3 He breaks the cruel power of sin,
   He sets the pris'ner free;
His blood can make the foulest clean;
   His blood avails for me.

4 He speaks, and listening to his voice,
   New life the dead receive;
The mournful, broken hearts rejoice;
   The humble poor believe.

124   Children of God.

1 How blest the children of the Lord,
   Who, walking in his sight,
Make all the precepts of his word
   Their study and delight.

2 Their works of piety and love
   Performed through Christ, their Lord,
Forever registered above,
   Shall meet a sure reward.

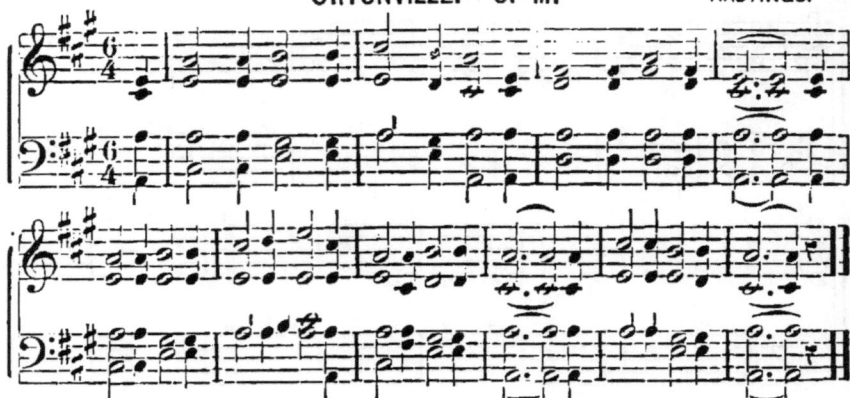

ORTONVILLE. C. M. — HASTINGS.

125   Word of God.

1 A glory in the Word we find,
  When grace restores our sight;
  But sin has darkened all the mind,
  And veiled the heavenly light.

2 When God's own Spirit clears our view,
  How bright the doctrines shine!
  Their holy fruits and sweetness show
  The Author is divine.

3 How blest are we, with open face
  To view thy glory, Lord,
  And all thy image here to trace,
  Reflected in thy word!

4 Oh! teach us, as we look, to grow
  In holiness and love,
  That we may long to see and know
  Thy glorious face above.

126   Sabbath Blessing.

1 Come, dearest Lord, and feed thy sheep,
  On this sweet day of rest;
  Oh! bless this flock, and make this fold
  Enjoy a heavenly rest.

2 Welcome and precious to my soul
  Are the sweet days of love;
  But what a Sabbath shall I keep
  When I shall rest above!

3 I come, I wait, I hear, I pray;
  Thy footsteps, Lord, I trace;
  Here, in thine own appointed way,
  I wait to see thy face.

4 Oh! if my soul, when Christ appears,
  In this sweet frame be found,
  I'll clasp my Saviour in mine arms,
  And leave this earthly ground.

127   Plenteous Grace.

1 Let plenteous grace descend on those
  Who, hoping in thy word,
  This day have solemnly declared
  That Jesus is their Lord.

2 With cheerful feet may they advance,
  And run the Christian race,
  And, through the troubles of the way,
  Find all-sufficient grace.

3 Lord, plant us all into thy death,
  That we thy life may prove—
  Partakers of thy cross beneath,
  And of thy crown above.

4 Come, Holy Spirit. Love divine,
  Thy grace to us be given;
  To a new life our souls incline,
  A life for God and Heaven.

128   Baptism.

1 Baptized into our Saviour's death
  Our souls to sin must die;
  With Christ our Lord we live anew,
  With Christ ascend on high.

2 There by his Father's side he sits,
  Enthroned divinely fair;
  Yet owns himself our Brother still,
  And our forerunner there.

3 Rise from these earthly trifles, rise
  On wings of faith and love;
  Above our choicest treasure lies,—
  And be our hearts above.

4 Let not earth's pleasures draw us down;
  Oh! give us strength to rise,
  And through thy strong, attractive power,
  At last to gain the prize.

129   Walk in the Light.

1 Walk in the light! so shalt thou know
  That fellowship of love
  His Spirit only can bestow,
  Who reigns in light above.

2 Walk in the light! and thou shalt own
  Thy darkness passed away;
  Because that light on thee hath shone
  In which is perfect day.

3 Walk in the light! and e'en the tomb
  No fearful shade shall wear;
  Glory shall chase away its gloom,
  For Christ hath conquered there.

4 Walk in the light! and thine shall be
  A path, though thorny, bright;
  For God, by grace, shall dwell in thee,
  And God himself is light.

ANTIOCH. C. M.

HANDEL.

130

1 Joy to the world, the Lord will come!
Let earth receive her King;
Let every heart prepare him room,
And Heav'n and nature sing.

2 Joy to the earth, the Lord will reign!
Let men their songs employ; [plains,
While fields and floods, rocks, hills, and
Repeat the sounding joy.

3 No more let sins and sorrows grow,
Nor thorns infest the ground;
He comes to make his blessings flow
Far as the curse is found.

4 Soon will he rule the earth with grace,
And make the nations prove
The glories of his righteousness,
And wonders of his love.

BRAY. C. M.

131 Impart Thy Blessing.

1 Within thy house, O Lord, our God,
In majesty appear;
Make this a place of thine abode,
And shed thy blessings here.

2 As we thy mercy-seat surround,
Thy Spirit, Lord, impart.

And let thy gospel's joyful sound
With power reach every heart,

3 Here let the blind their sight obtain;
Here give the mourner rest;
Let Jesus here triumphant reign,
Enthroned in every breast,

(81)

6

132   Love.

1 How sweet, how heavenly is the sight
  When those that love the Lord,
In one another's peace delight,
  And thus fulfill his word;

2 When each can feel his brother's sigh,
  And with him bear a part;
When sorrow flows from eye to eye,
  And joy from heart to heart;

3 When free from envy, scorn, and pride,
  Our wishes all above,
Each can his brother's failings hide
  And show a brother's love.

4 When love, in one delightful stream,
  Through every bosom flows;
And union sweet, and dear esteem,
  In every action glows.

133   Jesus, my Lord.

1 I'm not ashamed to own my Lord,
  Nor to defend his cause,
Maintain the honor of his word,
  The glory of his cross.

2 Jesus, my Lord, I know his name;
  His name is all my trust;
Nor will he put my soul to shame,
  Nor let my hope be lost.

3 Firm as his throne his promise stands,
  And he can well secure
What I've committed to his hands
  Till the decisive hour.

4 Then will he own my worthless name
  Before his Father's face,
And in the New Jerusalem
  Appoint my soul a place.

134   "Thy Word is Truth."

1 How shall the young secure their hearts,
  And guard their lives from sin?
Thy word the choicest rules imparts
  To keep the conscience clean.

2 'Tis like the sun, a heavenly light,
  That guides us all the day;
And through the dangers of the night,
  A lamp to lead our way.

(82)

3 Thy precepts make me truly wise;
  I hate the sinner's road;
I hate my own vain thoughts that rise,
  But love thy law, my God.

4 Thy word is everlasting truth;
  How pure is every page!
That holy book shall guide our youth,
  And well support our age.

135   Hope.

1 Dear as thou wert, and justly dear,
  We would not weep for thee;   [tear:
One thought shall check the starting
  From sorrow thou art free.

2 And thus shall faith's consoling power
  The tears of love restrain:
Oh, who that saw thy parting hour,
  Could wish thee back again?

3 Angels shall guard thy sleeping dust,
  And, as thy Saviour rose,
The grave again shall yield her trust,
  And end thy deep repose.

4 Thy Lord, before to glory gone,
  Shall bid thee come away;   [dawn
And calm and bright shall break the
  Of Heaven's eternal day.

136   Dedication.

1 To thee this temple we devote,
  Our Father and our God;
Accept it thine, and seal it now
  Thy Spirit's blest abode.

2 Here may the prayer of faith ascend,
  The voice of praise arise;
And may each lowly service prove
  Accepted sacrifice.

3 Here may the sinner learn his guilt,
  And weep before his Lord;
Here, pardoned, sing a Saviour's love,
  And here his vows record.

4 Peace be within these sacred walls;
  Prosperity be here;
Oh, smile upon thy people, Lord,
  And evermore be near.

WINTER. D. READ. Arr. by C. W. STONE.

I37 Guide My Ways.

1 Oh! that the Lord would guide my ways
  To keep his statutes still;
Oh! that my God would grant me grace
  To know and do his will.

2 O send thy Spirit down to write
  Thy law upon my heart;
Nor let my tongue indulge deceit,
  Nor act the liar's part.

3 From vanity turn off my eyes;
  Let no corrupt design,

Nor covetous desires, arise
  Within this soul of mine.

4 Order my footsteps by thy word,
  And make my heart sincere;
Let sin have no dominion, Lord,
  But keep my conscience clear.

5 Make me to walk in thy commands—
  'Tis a delightful road,
Nor let my head, nor heart, nor hands,
  Offend against my God.

COVENTRY. C. M. ARRANGED.

138 Brighter Scenes Above.

1 Oh! could our thoughts and wishes fly,
  Above these gloomy shades,
To those bright worlds beyond the sky,
  Where sorrow ne'er invades!

2 There, joys unseen by mortal eyes,
  Or reason's feeble ray,
In ever-blooming prospect rise,
  Exposed to no decay.

3 Lord, send a beam of light divine,
  To guide our upward aim!
With one reviving look of thine,
  Our languid hearts inflame.

4 Oh! then, on faith's sublimest wing,
  Our ardent souls shall rise, [spring,
To those bright scenes, where pleasures
  Immortal in the skies.

HARVEY'S CHANT. C. M.

139   Reverence.

1 With rev'rence let the saints appear,
   And bow before the Lord;
His high commands with rev'rence hear,
   And tremble at his word.

2 How terrible thy glories be!
   How bright thine armies shine!
Where is the power that vies with thee,
   Or truth compared with thine?

3 Sing, all ye ransomed of the Lord,
   Your great Deliv'rer sing;
Ye pilgrims now for Zion bound,
   Be joyful in your King.

4 O Jesus, Lord of earth and Heaven,
   Our life and joy, to thee
Be honor, thanks, and blessing given
   Through all eternity.

140   My Redeemer Liveth.

1 I know that my Redeemer lives,
   And ever prays for me;
A token of his love he gives,
   A pledge of liberty.

2 Jesus, I hang upon thy word,
   I steadfastly believe
Thou wilt return, and claim me, Lord,
   And to thyself receive.

3 Joyful in hope, my spirit soars
   To meet thee from above;
Thy goodness thankfully adores,—
   And sure I taste thy love.

4 When God is mine, and I am his,
   Of Paradise possessed,
I taste unutterable bliss,
   And everlasting rest.

141   How Happy They.

1 How happy they who know the Lord,—
   With whom he deigns to dwell!
He cheers and guides them by his word,
   His arm supports them well

2 His presence sweetens all their cares,
   And makes their burdens light,
A word from him dispels their fears,
   And gilds the gloom of night

142   Nearness to God.

1 Oh! could I find, from day to day,
   A nearness to my God,
Then would my hours glide sweet away,
   While leaning on his word.

2 Lord, I desire with thee to live
   Anew from day to day,
In joys the world can never give,
   Nor ever take away.

3 Blest Jesus, come, and rule my heart,
   And make me wholly thine,
That I may never more depart,
   Nor grieve thy love divine.

143   Thy Will be Done.

1 I ask not, Lord, for less to bear
   Here in the narrow way,
But that I may thy blessing share
   In all I do or say.

2 Through whatsoe'er my path shall lie,
   With patience may I run;
With filial trust my heart reply,
   Thy will, O God, be done.

3 With thee to lead, I will not fear
   In scenes with dangers rife,
While still thy cheering voice I hear,
   I am the way, the life.

4 Then help me to improve, with care,
   These precious moments given,
For they a faithful record bear,
   Of good or ill, to Heaven.

5 And in thine arms of love, enfold
   Me from the tempter's snare,
And in the book of life, enrolled,
   Be my name written there

144   Closing Hymn.

1 Now to the Lamb that once was slain,
   Be endless blessings paid;
Salvation, glory, joy, remain
   Forever on thy head.

2 Thou wilt redeem us by thy blood,
   And set the prisoners free,
And make us kings and priests to God,
   And we shall reign with thee.

VARINA. C. M. DOUBLE.
G. F. ROOT.

145   The Heavenly Land.

1 There is a land of pure delight,
    Where saints immortal reign;
Infinite day excludes the night,
    And pleasures banish pain.
There everlasting spring abides,
    And never-withering flowers,
And but a little space divides
    This heavenly land from ours.

2 Oh! could we make our doubts remove,
    Those gloomy doubts that rise,
And see the Canaan that we love,
    With unbeclouded eyes.—
Could we but climb where Moses stood,
    And view the landscape o'er,—
Not all this world's pretended good
    Could ever charm us more.

146   I Seek Thy Face.

1 Early, my God, without delay,
    I haste to seek thy face;
My thirsty spirit faints away
    Without thy cheering grace.
So pilgrims on the scorching sand,
    Beneath a burning sky,
Long for a cooling stream at hand,
    And they must drink or die.

2 I've seen thy glory and thy power
    Through all thy temple shine;
My God, repeat that heavenly hour,
    That vision so divine.
Not life itself, with all its joys,
    Can my best passions move,
Or raise so high my cheerful voice,
    As thy forgiving love.

147   Expectation.

1 The glories of that heavenly land,
    I've ofttimes felt before;
But what I feel is just a taste,
    And makes me long for more.
Had I the pinions of a dove,
    I'd fly and be at rest:
Then would I go to Christ, my love,
    And dwell among the blest.

2 Oh! could I reach my heavenly home,
    And ne'er return again;
I would not think the seasons long,
    That I should suffer pain.
But Patience bids us wait awhile!
    The crown's for them that fight;
The prize for those that win the race
    By faith, and not by sight.

148   Invitation.

1 Come to the living waters, come!
    Obey your Maker's call;
Return, ye weary wanderers, home,
    My grace is free for all.
Nothing ye in exchange shall give,
    Leave all you have behind;
Freely the gift of God receive,
    And peace in Jesus find.

2 I bid you all my goodness prove,
    My promises are free;
Come, taste the manna of my love,
    Delight your souls in me.
Your willing ear and heart incline,
    My words in faith receive,
Quickened, your souls by faith divine,
    Eternal life shall live.

149   Devotion.

1 I love to steal awhile away
    From every cumb'ring care,
And spend the hours of setting day
    In humble, grateful prayer.
I love, in solitude, to shed
    The penitential tear,
And all his promises to plead,
    Where none but God can hear.

2 I love to think of mercies past,
    And future good implore,
And all my cares and sorrows cast
    On him whom I adore.
I love, by faith, to take a view
    Of brighter scenes to come,
The prospect doth my strength renew
    While here away from home.

BADEA. S. M.　　GERMAN MELODY.

150　　The Sabbath.

1 Thy holy Sabbath, Lord,
　Thy people hail with joy;
And while we wait to hear thy word,
　Let praise our hearts employ.

2 With sweet delight, the day
　That thou hast called thine own,
We hail, and all our homage pay
　To thine exalted throne.

3 Oh! may thy saints be blest;
　Assist us while we pray;
May we enjoy a holy rest,
　And keep the sacred day.

4 When Sabbaths here shall end,
　And from these courts we move,
May we an endless Sabbath spend
　In heavenly courts above.

151　　Penitence.

1 Did Christ o'er sinners weep?
　And shall our cheeks be dry?
Let floods of penitential grief
　Burst forth from every eye.

2 The Son of God in tears,
　The wond'ring angels see!
Be thou astonished, O my soul!
　He shed those tears for thee.

3 He wept that we might weep;
　Each sin demands a tear;
In Heaven alone no sin is found,
　And there's no weeping there.

152　　Equip Me.

1 Equip me for the war,
　And teach my hands to fight;
My simple, upright heart prepare,
　And guide my words aright.

2 Control my every thought;
　My whole of sin remove;
Let all my works in thee be wrought,
　Let all be wrought in love.

3 Oh, arm me with the mind,
　Meek Lamb, that was in thee!
And let my knowing zeal be joined
　With perfect charity.

4 With calm and tempered zeal
　Let me enforce thy call;
And vindicate thy gracious will,
　Which offers life to all.

5 Oh, may I learn the art,
　With meekness to reprove!
To hate the sin with all my heart,
　But still the sinner love.

153　　God's Care.

1 How holy God's commands!
　How just his precepts are!
Come, cast your burdens on the Lord,
　And trust his constant care.

2 Beneath his watchful eye
　His saints securely dwell;
That hand which bears all nature up,
　Shall guard his children well.

3 Why should this anxious load
　Press down your weary mind?
Haste to your Heavenly Father's throne,
　And sweet refreshment find.

4 His goodness stands approved
　Through each succeeding day;
I'll drop my burden at his feet,
　And bear a song away.

154　　Bless the Lord.

1 Oh, bless the Lord, my soul!
　Let all within me join,
And aid my tongue to bless his name,
　Whose favors are divine.

2 He fills the poor with good:
　He gives the sufferers rest;
The Lord hath judgments for the proud,
　And justice for th' oppressed.

155　　Closing Hymn.

1 Lord, at this closing hour,
　Establish every heart
Upon thy word of truth and power,
　To keep us when we part.

2 Peace to our brethren give;
　Fill all our hearts with love;
In faith and patience may we live,
　And seek our rest above.

(86)

DOVE. S. M.

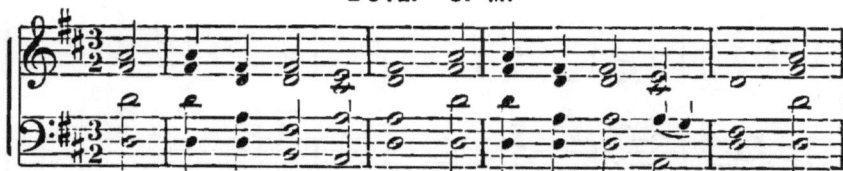

156 · Bless the Lord.

1 Stand up and bless the Lord,
  Ye people of his choice;
Stand up, and bless the Lord your God,
  With heart, and soul, and voice.

2 Though high above all praise,
  Above all blessing high,
Who would not fear his holy name,
  And laud and magnify?

3 Oh! for the living flame
  From his own altar brought,
To touch our lips, our souls inspire,
  And wing to Heaven our thought!

4 God is our strength and song,
  And his salvation ours;
Then be his love in Christ proclaimed
  With all our ransomed power.

157 · God's Law.

1 God's holy law, transgressed,
  Speaks nothing but despair;
Burdened with guilt, with grief oppres'd,
  We find no comfort there.

2 Not all our groans and tears,
  Nor works which we have done,
Nor vows, nor promises, nor prayers,
  Can e'er for sin atone.

3 Relief alone is found
  In Jesus' precious blood:
'Tis this that heals the mortal wound,
  And reconciles to God.

4 High lifted on the cross,
  The spotless Victim dies;
This is salvation's only source,
  Whence all our hopes arise.

158 The Better Land.

1 Beyond this gloomy night
  Eternal beauties rise,
A land of love, a land of light,
  Unseen by mortal eyes.

2 This is the land of life,
  Where death is known no more;
Saints ever rest, now free from strife,
  Their present labors o'er.

3 From sorrow, toil, and pain,
  And sin, we shall be free;
And perfect love and friendship reign
  Through all eternity.

159 Soldiers of Christ.

1 Soldiers of Christ, arise,
  And put your armor on;
Fight, for the battle will be ours;
  We fight to win a crown.

2 We fight not against flesh;
  We wrestle not with blood;
But principalities and powers,
  And for the truth of God;

3 With wicked spirits, too,
  That in high places stand,
Perverting oft the word of God,
  And say 'tis by command.

4 Put all the armor on,
  Like valiant soldiers stand;
Let all your loins be girt with truth,
  Waiting our Lord's command.

5 While Jesus is our friend,
  And his rich grace supplies,
We'll march like valiant soldiers on;
  We're sure to win the prize.

6 The battle's almost o'er;
  The race is nearly run;
Then with our glorious, conq'ring King,
  We'll sit down on his throne.

160 God's Bounty.

1 My Maker and my King,
  To thee my all I owe;
Thy sov'reign bounty is the spring
  Whence all my blessings flow.

2 The creature of thy hand,
  On thee alone I live;
My God, thy benefits demand
  More praise than I can give.

3 Lord, what can I impart,
  When all is thine before?
Thy love demands a thankful heart;
  The gift, alas! how poor.

ST. THOMAS. S. M.

A. WILLIAMS.

161   God's Word.

1 How perfect is thy Word,
   Thy judgments all are just;
And ever in thy promise, Lord,
   May man securely trust.

2 I hear thy word in love,
   In faith thy word obey;
Oh! send thy Spirit from above,
   To teach me, Lord, thy way.

3 Thy counsels all are plain,
   Thy precepts all are pure;
And long as Heaven and earth remain,
   The truth shall still endure.

4 Oh! may my soul with joy
   Trust in thy faithful word;
Be it through life my glad employ,
   To keep thy precepts, Lord.

162   Faith in Christ.

1 With willing hearts we tread
   The path the Saviour trod;
We love th' example of our Head,
   The glorious Lamb of God.

2 On thee, on thee alone,
   Our hope and faith rely,
O thou who wilt for sin atone,
   Who didst for sinners die!

3 We trust thy sacrifice;
   To thy dear cross we flee;
Oh! may we die to sin, and rise
   To life and bliss in thee.

163   Come, Holy Spirit.

1 Come, Holy Spirit, come;
   Let thy bright beams arise;
Dispel the sorrow from our minds,
   The darkness from our eyes.

2 Convince us of all sin;
   Then lead to Jesus' blood,
And to our wondering view reveal
   The mercies of our God.

3 Revive our drooping faith,
   Our doubts and fears remove,
And kindle in our breasts the flame
   Of never-dying love.

4 'Tis thine to cleanse the heart,
   To sanctify the soul,
To pour fresh life in every part,
   And new create the whole.

5 Come, Holy Spirit, come;
   Our minds from bondage free;
Then shall we know, and praise, and love
   The Father, Son, and thee.

164   Christ's Return.

1 In expectation sweet,
   We'll wait, and sing, and pray,
Till Christ's triumphal car we meet,
   And see an endless day.

2 He comes! The conq'ror comes!
   Death falls beneath his sword;
The joyful pris'ners burst the tombs,
   And rise to meet their Lord.

3 The trumpet sounds, Awake!
   The saints the call obey;
Their joyful upward flight they take,
   To realms of endless day.

4 Thrice happy morn for those
   Who love the ways of peace;
No night of sorrow e'er shall close,
   Or shade their perfect bliss.

165   Awake from Slumber.

1 Gracious Redeemer, shake
   This slumber from my soul!
Say to me now, Awake, awake,
   And Christ shall make thee whole.

2 Give me on thee to call,
   Always to watch and pray,
Lest I into temptation fall,
   And cast my shield away.

3 Oh! do thou always warn
   My soul of evil near!
When to the right or left I turn,
   Thy voice still let me hear:

4 Come back! this is the way!
   Come back! and walk therein!
Oh! may I hearken and obey,
   And shun the paths of sin!

VERMONT. S. M.

C. W. STONE.

166   God is Love.

1 There is a blessed hope,
    More precious and more bright
Than all the joyless mockery
    The world esteems delight.

2 There is a lovely star,
    That lights the darkest gloom,
And sheds a peaceful radiance o'er
    The prospects of the tomb.

3 There is a cheering voice,
    That lifts the soul above,
Dispels the painful, anxious doubt,
    And whispers, God is love.

4 That voice from Calvary's hight,
    Proclaims the soul forgiven;
That star is revelation's light;
    That hope, the hope of Heaven

167   Consecration.

1 Lord, in the strength of grace,
    With a glad heart, and free,
Myself, my residue of days,
    I consecrate to thee.

2 Thy willing servant, I
    Restore to thee thine own;
And from this moment, live or die,
    Will serve my God alone.

SHIRLAND. S. M.

STANLEY.

Glowing.

168   Evening Hymn.

1 The day is past and gone,
    The evening shades appear;
Oh! may we all remember well,
    The night of death draws near.

2 Lord, keep us safe this night,
    Secure from all our fears;
May angels guard us while we sleep,
    Till morning light appears.

3 And if we early rise,
    And view th' unwearied sun,
May we set out to win the prize,
    And after glory run.

4 And when our days are past,
    And we from time remove,
Oh! may we in thy bosom rest—
    The bosom of thy love.

(89)

LABAN. S. M.

L. MASON

169   Be on Thy Guard.

1 My soul, be on thy guard,
   Ten thousand foes arise;
The hosts of sin are pressing hard
   To draw me from the skies.

2 Oh! watch, and fight and pray;
   The battle ne'er give o'er;
Renew it boldly every day,
   And help divine implore.

3 Ne'er think the victory won,
   Nor lay thine armor down;
Thy arduous task will not be done
   Till thou obtain a crown.

170   Baptism.

1 Here, Saviour, we would come,
   In thine appointed way;
Obedient to thy high commands,
   Our solemn vows we pay.

2 Oh! bless this sacred rite,
   To bring us near to thee;
And may we find that as our day
   Our strength may also be.

171   The Lord's Supper.

1 Jesus invites his saints
   To meet around his board,
And sup in mem'ry of the death
   And sufferings of their Lord.

2 We take the bread and wine,
   As emblems of thy death;
Lord, raise our souls above the sign,
   To feast on thee by faith.

3 Faith eats the bread of life,
   And drinks the living wine,
It looks beyond this scene of strife—
   Unites us to the Vine.

4 Soon shall the night be gone,
   Our Lord will come again;
The marriage supper of the Lamb
   Will usher in his reign.

172   Jesus, my Hope.

1 Jesus, my strength, my hope,
   On thee I cast my care,
With humble confidence look up,
   And know thou hear'st my prayer.

2 I want a sober mind,
   A self-renouncing will,
That tramples down and casts behind
   The baits of pleasing ill:

3 A soul inured to pain,
   To hardship, grief, and loss;
Bold to take up, firm to sustain
   The consecrated cross.

4 I want a godly fear,
   A quick, discerning eye,
That looks to thee when sin is near,
   And sees the tempter fly

5 A spirit still prepared,
   And armed with jealous care,
Forever standing on its guard,
   And watching unto prayer.

173   Weigh not Thy Life.

1 My soul, weigh not thy life
   Against thy heavenly crown;
Nor suffer Satan's deadliest strife
   To beat thy courage down.

2 With prayer and crying strong,
   Hold on the fearful fight,
And let the breaking day prolong
   The wrestling of the night.

3 The battle soon will yield,
   If thou thy part fulfill;
For strong as is the hostile shield,
   Thy sword is stronger still.

4 Thine armor is divine,
   Thy feet with victory shod;
And on thy head shall quickly shine
   The diadem of God

174   The Pure in Heart.

1 Blest are the pure in heart,
   For they shall see our God,
The secret of the Lord is theirs;
   Their soul is his abode.

2 Still to the lowly soul,
   He doth himself impart,
And for his temple and his throne
   Selects the pure in heart.

175 .Jesus Comes.

1 Hark! that shout of rapture high,
    Bursting forth from yonder cloud;
Jesus comes, and, through the sky,
    Angels tell their joy aloud.

2 Hark! the trumpet's awful voice
    Sounds abroad o'er sea and land;
Let his people now rejoice;   .
    Their redemption is at hand.

3 See, the Lord appears in view;
    Heaven and earth before him fly;
Rise, ye saints, he comes for you;
    Rise, to meet him in the sky.

176 Soldier of the Cross.

1 Sleep not, soldier of the cross,
    Foes are lurking all around;
Look not here to find repose,
    This is but a battle-ground.

2 Up, and take thy shield and sword;
    Up, it is the call of Heaven:
Shrink not faithless from thy Lord,
    Nobly strive as he hath striven.

3 Break through all the force of ill,
    Tread the might of passion down,
Struggle onward, onward still,
    To the conquering Saviour's crown.

4 Through the midst of toil and pain,
    Let the tho't ne'er leave thy breast,
Every triumph thou dost gain
    Makes more sweet thy coming rest.

177 , Exaltation.

1 Magnify Jehovah's name!
    For his mercies, ever sure,
From eternity the same,
    To eternity endure.

2 Let his ransomed flock rejoice,
    Gathered out of every land,
As the people of his choice,
    Plucked from the destroyer's hand,

3 To the Lord their God they cry
    He inclines a gracious ear,
Sends deliverance from on high,
    Rescues them from all their fear.

4 Oh, that men would praise the Lord
    For his goodness to their race;
For the wonders of his word,
    And the riches of his grace!

178   Praise the Lord.

1 All ye nations, praise the Lord,
    All ye lands, your voices raise;
Heaven and earth, with loud accord,
    Praise the Lord, forever praise.

2 Praise him, ye who know his love,
    Praise him from the depths beneath;
Praise him in the heights above;
    Praise your Maker, all that breathe.

179   Meet Again.

1 Meet again when time is o'er,
    Meet again to part no more;
How it cheers the drooping heart,
    When from friends we're called to part.

2 Meet again where endless joy
    We shall taste without alloy;
Meet where songs shall ne'er grow old.
    Sweetly tuned to harps of gold.

3 Meet again, how passing sweet,
    Friends long lost again to meet;
Careworn souls, by tempest driven,
    Oh, how sweet to meet in Heaven!

180   Invitation.

1 Come, saith Jesus' sacred voice,
    Come, and make my paths your choice;
I will guide you to your home;
    Weary pilgrim, hither come.

2 Hither come; for here is found
    Balm for every bleeding wound,
Peace which ever shall endure,
    Rest, eternal, sacred, sure.

181   Closing Hymn.

1 Christian brother, ere we part, ·
    Every voice and every heart
Join, and to our Father raise
    One last hymn of grateful praise.

2 Though we here should meet no more,
    Yet there is a brighter shore;
There released from toil and pain,
    There we all may meet again.

HOLLY. 7s.

GEO. HEWS.

182   Consecration.

1 When, my Saviour, shall I be
Perfectly resigned to thee?
Poor and vile in my own eyes,
Only in thy wisdom wise?

2 Only thee content to know,
Ignorant of all below?
Only guided by thy light?
Only mighty in thy might?

3 Fully in my life express
All the hights of holiness; .
Sweetly let my spirit prove
All the depths of humble love.

183   Protection.

1 God of love that hearest prayer,
Kindly for thy people care,
Who on thee alone depend;
Love us, save us, to the end.

2 Save us in the prosperous hour,
From the flattering tempter's power,
From his unsuspected wiles,
From the world's pernicious smiles.

3 Cut off our dependence vain
On the help of feeble man;
Every arm of flesh remove;
Stay us only on thy love!

4 Never let the world break in;
Fix a mighty gulf between:
Keep us little and unknown,
Prized and loved by God alone.

184   Holy Bible.

1 Holy Bible! book divine!
Precious treasure, thou art mine!
Mine, to tell me whence I came;
Mine, to teach me what I am;

2 Mine, to chide me when I rove;
Min , to show a Saviour's love;
Mine, art thou to guide my feet;
Mine, to judge, condemn, acquit;

(92)

3 Mine, to comfort in distress,
If the Holy Spirit bless;
Mine, to show, by living faith,
Man can triumph over death;

4 Mine, to tell of joys to come,
And the rebel sinner's doom;
O thou holy book divine!
Precious treasure, thou art mine

185   Holy Spirit.

1 Holy Spirit, light divine,
Shine upon this heart of mine;
Chase the shades of night away,
Turn the darkness into day.

2 Holy Spirit, joy divine,
Cheer this saddened heart of mine;
Bid my many woes depart;
Heal my wounded, bleeding heart.

4 Holy Spirit, all divine,
Dwell within this heart of mine;
Cast down every idol throne;
Reign supreme, and reign alone.

186   Lov'st Thou Me?

1 Hark, my soul, it is the Lord;
'Tis the Saviour; hear his word;
Jesus speaks and speaks to thee,
Say, poor sinner, lov'st thou me?

2 I delivered thee when bound,
And when wounded, healed thy wound;
Sought thee wandering, set thee right,
Turned thy darkness into light.

3 Can a mother's tender care
Cease toward the child she bare?
Yes, she may forgetful be;
Yet will I remember thee.

4 Thou shalt see my glory soon,
When the work of grace is done;
Partner of my throne shalt be;
Say, poor sinner, lov'st thou me?

5 Lord, it is my chief complaint,
That my love's so weak and faint;
Yet, I love thee, and adore;
Oh, for grace to love thee more!

GREENVILLE. 8s & 7s. DOUBLE.

J. J. ROUSSEAU.

187   Waiting.

1 Long upon the mountains, weary,
   Have the scattered flock been torn;
   Dark the desert paths, and dreary,—
   Grievous trials have they borne.
   Now the gathering call is sounding,
   Solemn in its warning voice;
   Union, faith, and love, abounding,
   Bid the little flock rejoice.

2 Now the light of truth they're seeking,
   In its onward track pursue;
   All the ten commandments keeping,
   They are holy, just, and true.
   On the words of life they're feeding,
   Precious to their taste so sweet;
   All their Master's precepts heeding,
   Bowing humbly at his feet.

3 Soon He comes! with clouds descending;
   All his saints, entombed, arise;
   The redeemed in anthems blending
   Shouts of vict'ry through the skies.
   Oh! we long for thine appearing;
   Come, O Saviour! quickly come!
   Blessed hope! our spirits cheering,
   Take thy ransomed children home.

188   Our Home.

1 This is not my place of resting—
   Mine's a city yet to come;
   Onward, to it, I am hasting—
   On to my eternal home.
   In it, all is light and glory;
   O'er it shines a nightless day;
   Every trace of sin's sad story,
   All the curse hath passed away.

2 There the Lamb, our Shepherd, leads us
   By the streams of life along;
   On the freshest pastures feeds us,
   Turns our sighing into song.
   Soon we pass this desert dreary,
   Soon we bid farewell to pain;
   Never more are sad and weary,
   Never, never sin again.

189   Thy Kingdom Come.

1 Come, thou long-expected Jesus,
   Born to set thy people free;
   From our fears and sins release us,
   Let us find our rest in Thee;
   Israel's strength and consolation,
   Hope of all the saints thou art;
   Dear Desire of every nation,
   Joy of every longing heart.

2 Born, thy people to deliver;
   Born a child and yet a King;
   Born to reign o'er us forever,
   Now thy precious kingdom bring;
   By thine own eternal Spirit,
   Rule in all our hearts alone;
   By thine all-sufficient merit,
   Raise us to thy glorious throne.

190   Guard Us.

1 Gracious Father, guard thy children
   From the foe's destructive power;
   Save, oh, save them, Lord, from falling
   In this dark and trying hour.
   Thou wilt surely prove thy people,
   All our graces must be tried;
   But thy word illumes our pathway,
   And in God we still confide.

2 We are in the time of waiting;
   Soon we shall behold our Lord,
   Wafted far away from sorrow,
   To receive our rich reward.
   Keep us, Lord, till thine appearing,
   Pure, unspotted from the world;
   Let thy holy Spirit cheer us,
   Till thy banner is unfurled.

3 With what joyful exultation
   Shall the saints thy banner see,
   When the Lord for whom we've waited,
   Shall proclaim the Jubilee!
   Freedom from this world's pollutions;
   Freedom from all sin and pain;
   Freedom from the wiles of Satan,
   And from death's destructive reign.

191 ⸝ Sabbath Praise.

1 Safely through another week,
  God has brought us on our way;
Let us now a blessing seek,
  Waiting in his courts to-day:
Day of all the week the best!
Emblem of eternal rest!

2 While we seek supplies of grace,
  Through the dear Redeemer's name,
Show thy reconciling face,
  Take away our sin and shame;
From our worldly cares set free,
May we rest this day in thee.

3 Here we come, thy name to praise;
  May we feel thy presence near;
May thy glory meet our eyes
  While we in thy courts appear;
Here afford us, Lord, a taste
Of our everlasting feast.

4 May thy gospel's joyful sound
  Conquer sinners, comfort saints;
Make the fruits of grace abound,
  Bring relief for all complaints:
Thus may all our Sabbaths be,
Till we rise to reign with thee.

192 ⸝ Saviour, Pilot Me.

1 Jesus, Saviour, pilot me
  Over life's tempestuous sea;
Unknown waves before me roll,
Hiding rock and treacherous shoal:
Chart and compass came from thee;
Jesus, Saviour, pilot me.

2 When the apostle's fragile bark
Struggled with the billows dark,
On the stormy Galilee,
Thou didst walk upon the sea;
And when they beheld thy form,
Safe they glided through the storm.

3 When at last I near the shore,
  And the fearful breakers roar
'Tween me and the peaceful rest,
Then, while leaning on thy breast,
May I hear thee say to me,
Fear not, I will pilot thee.

193 Rock of Ages.

1 Rock of ages, cleft for me,
  Let me hide myself in thee;
Let the water and the blood,
From thy wounded side that flowed,
Be of sin the perfect cure:
Save me, Lord, and make me pure.

2 Should my tears forever flow,
  Should my zeal no languor know,
This, for sin, could not atone:
Thou must save and thou alone.
In my hand no price I bring;
Simply to thy cross I cling.

3 When my pilgrimage I close,
  Victor o'er the last of foes,
When I soar to worlds unknown,
See thee on thy judgment throne,
Rock of ages, cleft for me,
Let me hide myself in thee.

194 Social Worship.

1 If 'tis sweet to mingle where
Christians meet for social prayer,
If 'tis sweet, with them to raise
Songs of holy joy and praise,
Oh, how sweet that state must be,
Where they meet eternally!

2 Saviour, may these meetings prove
Preparations from above;
While we worship in this place,
May we go from grace to grace,
Till we each, in his degree,
Fit for endless glory be.

195. Closing Sabbath.

1 Closing Sabbath! Ah, how soon
  Have thy sacred moments passed:
Scarcely shines the morn. the noon,
  Ere the evening brings thy last!
    And another Sabbath flies—
    Solemn witness! to the skies!

2 What is the report it bears
  To the secret place of God?
Does it speak of worldly cares,
  Thoughts which cling to earth's low sod?
    Or has sweet communion shone
    Through its hours from God alone?

3 Could we hope the day was spent
  Prayerfully, with constant heart,
We might yield it up content—
  Knowing though so soon it part,
    We should see a better day,
    Which could never pass away.

4 God of Sabbaths! oh, forgive!
  That we use thy gifts so ill;
Teach us daily how to live,
  That we ever may fulfill
    All thy gracious love designed,
    Giving Sabbaths to mankind.

FREEPORT. 10s.

196. The Sabbath.

1 Again the day returns of holy rest, [blest;
Which, when he made the world, Jehovah
When, like his own, he bade our labors
And all be piety, and all be peace. [cease,

2 Let us devote this consecrated day
To learn his will, and all we learn obey;
So shall he hear, when fervently we raise
Our supplications, and our songs of praise.

3 Lord of all worlds! incline thy bounteous
    ear:
Thy children's voice in tender mercy
    hear;
Bear thy blest promise, fixed as hills, in
    mind,
And shed renewing grace on lost mankind.

4 Father in Heaven! in whom our hopes
    confide,
Whose power defends us, and whose
    precepts guide;
Through life our surest guardian and
    friend,
Glory supreme be thine till time shall
    end.

197. Hail, Happy Day.

1 Hail, happy day! thou day of holy rest—
What heavenly peace and transport fill
    our breast!
When Christ, the Lord of grace, in love
    descends,
And kindly holds communion with his
    friends.

2 Let earth and all its vanities be gone,
Move from my sight, and leave my soul
    alone;
Its flattering, fading glories, I despise,
And to immortal beauties turn my eyes.

3 Fain would I mount and penetrate the
    skies,
And on my Saviour's glories fix my eyes:
Oh! meet my rising soul, thou God of
    love,
And waft it to the blissful realms above!

4 O Son of God, exalted on thy throne,
Impart that grace which comes from thee
    alone:
Thou, by whose love our light and peace
    are given,
Bring us, dear Saviour, to thyself and
    Heaven.

PRAYER OF THE CHURCH. 7s & 6s.

198   How Long, O Lord?

1 How long, O Lord our Saviour,
   Wilt thou remain away?
Our hearts are growing weary
   Of thy so long delay.
Oh! when shall come the moment,
   When, brighter far than morn,
The sunshine of thy glory
   Shall on thy people dawn?

2 How long, O grac'ous Master,
   Wilt thou thy household leave?
So long hast thou now tarried,
   Few they return believe.
Immersed in sloth and folly,
   Thy servants, Lord, we see;
And few of us stand ready
   With joy to welcome thee.

3 Oh! wake thy slumbering people;
   Send forth the solemn cry;
Let all the saints repeat it,
   The Saviour draweth nigh!
May all our lamps be burning,
   Our loins well girded be,
Each longing heart preparing
   With joy thy face to see,

199   Help Each Other.

1 Speak often to each other,
   To cheer the fainting mind;
And often be your voices
   In pure devotion joined;
Though trials may await you,
   The crown before you lies;
Take courage, brother pilgrim,
   And soon you'll win the prize.

2 Ye shall be mine, says Jesus,
   In that auspicious day,
When I make up my jewels,
   Released from cumb'rous clay;

He'll polish and refine you
   From worthless dross and tin,
And to his heavenly kingdom,
   Will bid you enter in.

3 We'll range the wide dominion
   Of our Redeemer round,
And in dissolving raptures,
   Be lost in love profound;
While all the flaming harpers,
   Begin the lasting song,
With hallelujahs rolling
   From the unnumbered throng.

200   The Cleansing Blood.

1 The sprinkled blood is speaking
   Before the Father's throne,
The Spirit's power is seeking
   To make its virtues known.
The sprinkled blood is telling
   Jehovah's love to man,
While heavenly harps are swelling
   Sweet notes to mercy's plan.

2 The sprinkled blood is sparkling
   Forgiveness full and free,
Its wondrous power is breaking
   Each bond of guilt for me.
The sprinkled blood's revealing
   A Father's smiling face,
While Jesus' love is sealing
   Each monument of grace.

3 The sprinkled blood is pleading
   Its virtue as my own,
And there my soul is reading
   Her title to thy throne.
The sprinkled blood is owning
   The weak one's feeblest plea;
'Mid sighs, and tears, and groaning,
   It pleads, O Lord, with thee.

Oh, wondrous power that seeketh
    Fro a sin to set me face!
Ah, precious blood that speaketh!
    Should I not value thee?
The sprinkled blood is shedding
    Its fragrance all around,
It gilds the path we're treading,
    It makes our joys abound.

201   Day of Rest.

1 O day of rest and gladness,
    O day of joy and light,
O balm of care and sadness,
    Most beautiful, most bright;
On thee, the high and lowly,
    Bending before the throne,
Sing, Holy, holy, holy,
    To the Eternal One.

2 Thou art a port protected
    From storms that round us rise,
A garden intersected
    With streams of Paradise;
Thou art a cooling fountain
    In life's dry, dreary sand;
From thee, like Pisgah's mountain,
    We view our promised land.

3 A day of sweet reflection
    Thou art, a day of love;
A day to raise affection
    From earth to things above.

New graces ever gaining
    From this our day of rest,
We seek the rest remaining
    In mansions of the blest.

202   Better Riches.

1 Farewell, all earthly treasures
    I bid you all adieu;
· Farewell, all earthly honor,
    I want no more of you.
I want my union grounded
    On the eternal Son,
Beyond the power of Satan,
    Where sin can never come.

2 I want my name engraven
    Among the righteous ones,
Crying, Holy, holy Father,
    And wear a righteous crown.
For the sake of purer riches,
    I'm willing to pass through
All earthly tribulation,
    And count it my just due.

4 All earthly tribulation
    Is but a moment here;
And oh! if we are faithful,
    A crown of life we'll wear.
We shall be called holy,
    And feed on angels' food,
Rejoicing in bright glory
    Around the throne of God.

TO-DAY THE SAVIOUR CALLS. 6s & 4s.

203   To-Day.

1 To-day the Saviour calls!
    Ye wanderers, come!
O ye benighted souls,
    Why longer roam?

2 To-day the Saviour calls!
    Oh! listen now;
Within these sacred walls,
    To Jesus bow.

3 To-day the Saviour calls!
    For mercy flee;
For all the guilty soon
    Must guilty be.

4 To-day the Saviour calls!
    For refuge fly;
The storm of vengeance falls;
    Ruin is nigh.

5 The Spirit calls to-day!
    Yield to its power;
Oh! grieve it not away;
    'Tis mercy's hour.

204   The Better Day.

1 By faith I see the day
    That ends my woes,
When I shall vict'ry gain
    O'er all my foes.

2 In yonder realms of light,
    By faith I see
A crown of glory bright,
    Prepared for me.

3 Oh! may I ever keep
    The prize in view;
And through the storms of life
    My way pursue.

4 Jesus, be thou my guide;
    My steps attend;
Oh! keep me near thy side;
    Be thou my friend.

5 Be thou my shield and sun,
    Be thou my guard;
And, when my work is done,
    My great reward.

(97)

7

205   Supplication.

1 Let thy Spirit, blessed Saviour,
   Come and bid our doubtings cease;
Come, oh! come with love and favor,
   Fill us all with joy and peace.

2 Fearful dangers are around us,
   Satan watches to destroy;
Lord, our foes would fain confound us;
   Oh! for us thy might employ!

3 On thy word our souls are resting,
   Taught by thee, thy name we love;
Sweetest of all names is Jesus;
   How it doth our spirits move!

4 Let us not, O Lord, be weary
   Of the roughness of the way;
Though the road be often dreary,
   Thou shalt drive our gloom away.

206   Love Divine.

1 Love divine, all love excelling,
   Joy of Heaven to earth come down!
Fix in us thy humble dwelling;
   All thy faithful mercies crown.

2 Jesus! thou art all compassion,—
   Pure, unbounded love thou art;
Visit us with thy salvation,
   Enter every trembling heart.

3 Breathe, oh! breathe thy loving Spirit
   Into every troubled breast!
Let us all in thee inherit;
   Let us find thy promised rest.

4 Changed from glory into glory,
   Till in Heaven we take our place;
Till we cast our crowns before thee,
   Lost in wonder, love, and praise.

207   Praise.

1 Praise to thee, thou great Creator!
   Praise to thee from every tongue;
Join, my soul, with every creature,
   Join the universal song.

2 Father, source of all compassion,
   Pure, unbounded grace is thine:
Hail the God of our salvation,
   Praise him for his love divine!

(98)

3 For thy countless blessings given,
   For the hope of future joy,
Sound his name thro' earth and Heaven,
   Let his praise your tongues employ.

4 Joyfully on earth adore him,
   Till in Heaven our song we raise:
Then enraptured fall before him,
   Lost in wonder, love, and praise.

208   Missionary Hymn.

1 He that goeth forth with weeping,
   Bearing precious seed in love,
Never tiring, never sleeping,
   Findeth mercy from above.

2 Soft descend the dews of Heaven,
   Bright the rays celestial shine;
Precious fruits will thus be given,
   Through an influence all divine.

3 Sow thy seed, be never weary,
   Let no fears thy soul annoy;
Be the prospect ne'er so dreary,
   Thou shalt reap the fruits of joy.

4 Lo! the scene of verdure brightening!
   See the rising grain appear;
Look again! the fields are whitening,
   For the harvest-time is near.

209   God is our Strength.

1 Vain were all our toil and labor,
   Did not God that labor bless;
Vain, without his grace and favor,
   Every talent we possess.

2 Vainer still the hope of Heaven,
   That on human strength relies;
But to him shall help be given
   Who in humble faith applies.

210   Benediction.

1 May the grace of Christ, our Saviour,
   And the Father's boundless love,
With the Holy Spirit's favor,
   Rest upon us from above.

2 Thus may we abide in union
   With each other and the Lord,
And possess, in sweet communion,
   Joys which earth cannot afford.

211   **Beyond the River.**

1 I can see beyond the river,
    Over Jordan's dashing tide;
  There I'll be with Christ forever,
    By my Saviour's bleeding side.

2 Over there is no more weeping,
    Over there all pain is o'er;
  I shall rest in Jesus' keeping,
    I shall droop and die no more.

3 Over there is no more sinning,
    Over there are sunny skies;
  Crowns of fadeless beauty winning,
    Blooming flowers of Paradise.

4 Over there I'll find my treasure—
    Jewels lost long, long ago;

Love and bliss, in fullest measure.
    There my raptured heart shall know.

5 Over there all are immortal;
    Over there is no more night;
  And the city's pearly portal
    Now almost appears in sight.

212   **Closing Hymn.**

1 Praise the God of all creation;
    Praise the Father's boundless love;
  Praise the Lamb, our expiation,—
    Priest and King, enthroned above;

2 Praise the Fountain of salvation,—
    Him in whom his people live;
  Undivided adoration
    To the Lord Jehovah give.

THE SHINING SHORE. 8s & 7s. Peculiar.
GEO. F. ROOT.

213   **The Shining Shore.**

1 My days are gliding swiftly by,
    And I, a pilgrim stranger.
  Would not detain them as they fly—
    Those hours of toil and danger;
CHORUS.
    For, oh! we stand on Jordan's strand,
    And soon we'll all pass over;
    And just before the shining shore
    We may almost discover.

2 We'll gird our loins, my brethren dear,
    Our distant home discerning;
  Our absent Lord has left us word,
    Let every lamp be burning.

3 Should coming days be cold and dark,
    We need not cease our singing:
  That perfect rest naught can molest,
    Where golden harps are ringing.

4 Let sorrow's rudest tempests blow,
    Each cord on earth to sever, [home,
  Our King says, Come, and there's our
    Forever, oh! forever!

214   **Jesus our King.**

1 There is no name so sweet on earth,
    No name so sweet in Heaven,
  The name before his wondrous birth,
    To Christ, the Saviour, given.
CHORUS.
    We love to sing around our King,
    And hail him blessed Jesus;
    For there's no word ear ever heard,
    So dear, so sweet as Jesus.

2 He's now upon his Father's throne,
    Almighty to release us
  From sin and pains, he gladly reigns,
    The Prince and Saviour, Jesus.

ARIEL. C. P. M.   DR. MASON.

215   Matchless Worth.

1 Oh! could I speak the matchless worth,
Oh! could I sound the glories forth,
   Which in my Saviour shine,
I'd soar and touch the heavenly strings,
And vie with Gabriel while he sings,
   In notes almost divine.

2 I'd sing the character he bears,
And all the forms of love he wears,
   Exalted on his throne:
In loftiest songs of sweetest praise,
I would to everlasting days
   Make all his glories known.

3 Well, the delightful day will come,
When my dear Lord will take me home,
   And I shall see his face:
Then, with my Saviour, brother, friend,
A blest eternity I'll spend,
   Triumphant in his grace.

216   Shall I be There?

1 When thou, my righteous Judge, shalt
   come,
To call thy ransomed people home,
   Shall I among them stand?
Shall such a worthless worm as I,
Who sometimes am afraid to die,
   Be found at thy right hand?

2 I love to meet among them now,
Before thy gracious throne to bow,
   Though weakest of them all;
Nor can I bear the piercing thought,
To have my worthless name left out,
   When thou for them shalt call!

3 Prevent, prevent it by thy grace!
Be thou, dear Lord, my hiding-place
   In that expected day.

(100)

Thy pardoning voice, oh! let me hear,
To still each unbelieving fear,
   Nor let me fall, I pray.

4 Let me among thy saints be found,
Whene'er the Archangel's trump shall
   sound,
   To see thy smiling face;
Then loud through all the crowd I'll sing,
While Heaven's resounding mansions ring
   With shouts of endless grace.

217   Conversion.

1 O God, my inmost soul convert,
And deeply on my thoughtful heart
   Eternal things impress;
Cause me to feel their solemn weight,
And tremble on the brink of fate,
   And wake to righteousness.

2 Before me place in dread array
The pomp of that tremendous day,
   When thou with clouds shalt come
To judge the nations at thy bar;
And tell me, Lord, shall I be there,
   To meet a joyful doom?

3 Be this my one great business here,
With serious industry and fear,
   Eternal bliss t' insure—
Thy utmost counsel to fulfill,
And suffer all thy righteous will,
   And to the end endure.

4 Then, Father, then, my soul receive,
Transported from this vale, to live
   And reign with thee above,
Where faith is sweetly lost in sight,
And hope in full, supreme delight,
   And everlasting love.

AMERICA. 6s & 4s.

218   Break, Eternal Day.

1 Break, break, eternal day,
   Bid darkness flee away,
     Pour on our sight—
  Light from the world of joy,
  Bliss pure without alloy:
  Then ne'er shall gloom annoy,
     All shall be bright.

2 Rise, rise, thou glorious sun,
  Hasten thy race to run;
     At God's command,
  Extend thy healing wings,
  Open joy's long-sealed springs,
  Reign, O thou King of kings,
     In this dark land.

3 Come, come, thou conquering One,
  Reign thou upon thy throne,
     In glory bright;
  Then shall the ransomed raise,
  Unceasing songs of praise,
  Throughout eternal days,
     In realms of light.

219   Raise Your Voices.

1 Come, let our voices raise
  A song of grateful praise,
     And thankful love;
  Let each a tribute bring,
  Let all awake and sing,
  Praise to our heavenly King,
     Who dwells above.

2 The gospel's sacred page
  Reveals to every age
     Salvation free.
  Oh, send the joyful sound,
  And let it echo round,
  Till praises loud resound,
     O God, to thee!

3 Accept our offerings, Lord,
  To spread thy truth abroad,
     Our labors own!
  At length at thy right hand
  May we together stand,
  And with the angel band
     Surround thy throne!

OAK. 6s & 4s.

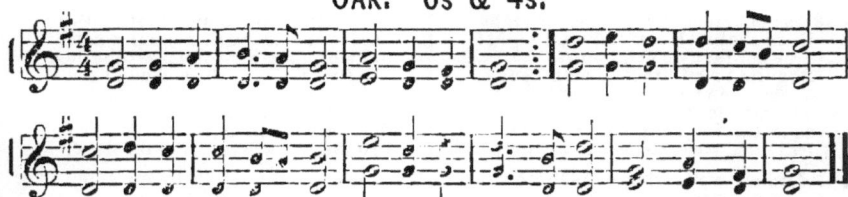

220   Heaven is my Home.

1 I'm but a stranger here,
  Heaven is my home;
  Earth is a desert drear,
  Heaven is my home.
  Danger and sorrow stand
  Round me on every hand;
  Heaven is my fatherland,
  Heaven is my home.

2 What though the tempest rage,
  Heaven is my home;
  Short is my pilgrimage;
  Heaven is my home.

Time's cold and wintry blast
  Soon will be overpast:
  I shall reach home at last,
  Heaven is my home.

3 There at my Saviour's side,
  Heaven is my home,
  I shall be glorified,
  Heaven is my home.
  There'll be the good and blest,
  Those I love most and best,
  There, too, I soon shall rest;
  Heaven is my home.

THE DREAM OF PILATE'S WIFE.

221 The Dream of Pilate's Wife.

1 It was not sleep that bound my sight
   Upon that well-remembered night;
It was not fancy's fitful power
   Beguiled me in that solemn hour.
But o'er the vision of my soul
   The mystic future seemed to roll;
And in the deep, prophetic trance,
   Revealed its treasures to my glance.

2 Before my wondering eyes there stood
   A vast, a countless multitude;
The hoary sire, the prattling child,
   The mother, and the maiden mild,
The gladsome youth, and man of care—
   All tribes, all ages, mingled there;
And all, where'er I turned to see,
   In humble silence bent the knee.

3 Still o'er the crowded scene I gazed;
   Against the lurid eastern sky
I saw the shameful cross upraised,
   I saw the sufferer doomed to die.
'Twas He whom late with sorrowing mien,
   In Zion's streets I oft had seen;
And now in blood and agony,
   He turned a dying look on me.

4 Then softly from that gathering throng
   Arose the sound of solemn song;
And while I caught the swelling lay,
   The myriad voices seemed to say—
And we believe in him that died,
   By Pontius Pilate crucified—
That he shall come, when time is fled,
   To judge the living and the dead.

5 I woke; thou wast not by my side,
   I heard a loud exulting cry:
I heard the scornful priests deride,
   The elders murmur, Crucify!
O Pilate! hadst thou marked my prayer,
   That guiltless blood to shield and spare,
That deed of horror would not be
   A stain to thine—a curse to thee!

6 Our scenes of early love are past;
   Our youthful spring is withered all;
Afar from Rome our lot is cast,
   Beneath the sunny skies of Gaul;
The thoughts that memory treasures yet
   Of other days, begin to flee;
But never shall my heart forget
   The Crucified of Galilee!

222 The Judgment.

1 Oh, solemn thought, and can it be
The hour of Judgment now is come,
Which soon must fix our destiny,
And seal the sinner's fearful doom?
Yes, it is so; the Judgment hour
Is swiftly hastening to its close:
Then will the Judge, in mighty power,
Descend in vengeance on his foes.

2 He who came down to earth to die,
An offering for the sins of men,
And then ascended up on high,
And will ere long return again,
Is standing now before the ark,
And mercy-seat, and cherubim,
To plead his blood for saints, and make
The last remembrance of their sin.

3 The solemn moment is at hand
When we who have his name confessed,
Each in his lot must singly stand,
And pass the final, searching test.
Jesus! we hope in thee alone;
In mercy now upon us look,
Confess our names before the throne,
And blot our sins from out thy book.

4 O blessed Saviour! may we feel
The full importance of this hour.
Inspire our hearts with holy zeal,
And aid us by thy Spirit's power;
That we may in thy strength be strong,
And brave the conflict valiantly;
Then, on Mount Zion, join the song,
And swell the notes of victory.

HAIL TO THE BRIGHTNESS. 11s & 10s.

223 Hail to the Brightness.

1 Hail to the brightness of Zion's glad
morning! [lain!
Joy to the lands that in darkness have
Hushed be the accents of sorrow and
mourning:
Zion, in triumph, begins her mild reign.

2 Lo, in the desert rich flowers are spring-
ing;
Streams ever copious are gliding along;
Loud, from the mountain-tops, echoes are
ringing; [song.
Wastes rise in verdure, and mingle in

3 See, the dead risen from land and from
ocean,
Praise to Jehovah, ascending on high;
Fall'n are the engines of war and commo-
tion,
Shouts of salvation are rending the sky.

224 Heir of the Kingdom.

1 Heir of the kingdom, oh! why dost thou
slumber [home?
Why art thou sleeping so near thy blest
Wake thee, arouse thee, and gird on thine
armor,
Speed, for the moments are hurrying on.

2 Heir of the kingdom, say, why dost thou
linger?
How canst thou tarry in sight of the prize?
Up, and adorn thee, the Saviour is com-
ing;
Haste to receive him descending the skies.

3 Earth's mighty nations, in strife and
commotion,
Tremble with terror and sink in dismay;
Listen, 'tis naught but the chariot's loud
rumbling;
Heir of the kingdom, no longer delay.

4 Stay not, oh! stay not for earth's vain al-
lurements;
See how its glory is passing away;
Break the strong fetters the foe hath
bound o'er thee;
Heir of the kingdom, turn, turn thee away.

5 Keep the eye single, the head upward
lifted; [King;
Watch for the glory of earth's coming
Lo! o'er the mountain-tops light is now
breaking; [sing.
Heirs of the kingdom, rejoice ye, and

MY REST IS IN HEAVEN. 11s.

225 **My Rest is in Heaven.**

1 My rest is in Heaven, my rest is not here,
Then why should I tremble when trials
    are near?   [can come,
Be hushed, my sad spirit, the worst that
But shortens my journey, and hastens
    me home.

2 It is not for me to be seeking my bliss,
Or building my hopes in a region like this;
I look for a city that hands have not piled,
I pant for a country by sin undefiled.

3 The thorn and the thistle around me may
    grow,
I would not lie down upon roses below;
I ask not my portion, I seek not my rest,
Till I find them forever on Jesus's breast.

4 Afflictions may press me, they cannot de-
    stroy,   [into joy;
One glimpse of his love turns them all
And the bitterest tears, if he smile but on
    them,   [and gem.
Like dew in the sunshine, grow diamond

5 Let doubt, then, and danger my progress
    oppose,   [its close;
They only make Heaven more sweet at
Come joy or come sorrow, whate'er may
    befall,   [them all.
An hour with my God will make up for

6 A scrip on my back, and a staff in my
    hand,   [land;
I march on in haste through an enemy's
The road may be rough, but it cannot be
    long;   [with song.
I'll smooth it with hope, and I'll cheer it

226 **I Love Thee.**

1 I love thee, I love thee, I love thee, my
    Lord;   [God;
I love thee, my Saviour; I love thee, my
I love thee, I love thee, and that thou
    dost know;   [will show.
But how much I love thee, my actions

2 I'm happy, I'm happy, oh! wondrous
    account!   (mount!
My joys are immortal, I stand on the
I gaze on my treasure, and long to be
    there,   (dear.
With Jesus and angels, and kindred so

3 O Jesus, my Saviour, with thee I am
    blest—
My life and salvation, my joy and my rest.
Thy name be my theme, and thy love be
    my song;   (and my tongue.
Thy grace shall inspire both my heart

4 Oh! who's like my Saviour? He's Salem's
    bright King;   (me to sing.
He smiles, and he loves me, and learns
I'll praise him, I'll praise him, with notes
    loud and clear,   (cheer.
While rivers of pleasure my spirit do

227 **I'm Weary.**

1 I'm weary of staying—oh! when shall I
    rest   (the blest;
In that promised land of the good and
Where sin can no longer her blandish-
    ments spread,   (fled?
And tears and temptations forever are

2 I'm weary of sighing o'er sorrows of
    earth,   (their birth;
O'er joy's glowing visions that fade at
O'er the pangs of the loved which we
    cannot assuage,   (weakness of age.
O'er the blightings of youth and the

3 I'm weary of hoping, where hope is un-
    true,   (dew;
As fair but as fleeting as bright morning
I long for that land whose blest promise
    alone   (throne.
Is changeless, and sure as eternity's

4 I'm weary of loving what passes away;
The sweetest and dearest, alas! may not
    stay;   (are o'er,
I long for that land where these partings
And death and the tomb can divide us no
    more!

BEAR ME ON.

Arr. by C. W. STONE.

228 **Bear Me On.**

1 Oh! how I long to see that day,
  When the redeemed shall come
To Zion, clad in white array—
  Their blissful, happy home.

Cho.—Oh! bear me on, bear me on
  To Mount Zion;
  · Then bear me on to that city of love,
  Where saints will ever dwell.

2 To hear the alleluias roll
  From the unnumbered throng:
The kingdom spread from pole to pole;
  And join redemption's song.

3 To see all Israel safe at home,
  Singing on Zion's hight;

And Jesus crowned upon his throne,
  Creation own his right.

4 All hail! the morn of glory's nigh,
  The pilgrim longs to see,
That dries the tear from every eye—
  Creation's jubilee.

5 Jerusalem I long to see,
  Blest city of my King;
And eat the fruit of life's fair tree,
  And hear the blood-washed sing.

6 My longing heart cries out, Oh, come!
  Creation groans for thee!
The weary pilgrim sighs, Oh, come!
  Bring immortality!

HERE IS NO REST. 10s &11s.

Fine.

D. C.

229 **Here is no Rest.**

1 Here o'er the earth as a stranger I roam,
  Here is no rest, is no rest;
Here as a pilgrim I wander alone,
  Yet I am blest, I am blest;
For I look forward to that glorious day,
When sin and sorrow will vanish away;

My heart doth leap while I hear Jesus say,
  There, there is rest, there is rest.

2 Here fierce temptations beset me around,
  Here is no rest, is no rest; (surround;
Here I am grieved while my foes me
  Yet I am blest, I am blest.
Let them revile me, and scoff at my name,
Laugh at my weeping—endeavor to
  shame;
I will go forward, for this my theme,
  There, there is rest, there is rest.

(105)

THE HEAVENLY MANSIONS.

We'll wait till Je-sus comes,

We'll wait till Je-sus comes, We'll wait till Je-sus comes, And we'll be gather'd home.

230 The Heavenly Mansion.

1 Let others seek a home below,
  We'll be gathered home;
  Which flames devour or waves o'erflow
  We'll be gathered home.

2 Be mine the happier lot to own,
  We'll be gathered home;
  A heavenly mansion near the throne,
  We'll be gathered home.

3 Then, fail this earth, let stars decline,
  We'll be gathered home;
  And sun and moon refuse to shine,
  We'll be gathered home.

4 Though desolation here may be,
  We'll be gathered home;
  That heavenly mansion stands for me,
  We'll be gathered home.

HOMEWARD BOUND. 10s & 7s.

FINE.

D. C.

231   Homeward Bound.

1 Out on the ocean all boundless we ride,
  We're homeward bound, homeward
  bound;   [tide,
  Tossed on the waves of a rough, restless
  We're homeward bound, homeward
  bound.   [rode,
  Far from the safe, quiet harbor, we've
  Seeking our Father's celestial abode,
  Promise of which on us each he bestow'd,
  We're homeward bound, homeward
  bound.

2 Wildly the storm sweeps us on as it roars,
  We're homeward bound, homeward
  bound;   [shores,
  Look! yonder lie the bright, heavenly
  We're homeward bound, homeward
  bound.
  Steady, O pilot! stand firm at the wheel:
  Steady, we soon shall outweather the
  gale;   [sail,
  Oh! how we fly 'neath the loud-creaking
  We're homeward bound, homeward
  bound.

3 Into the harbor of Heaven now we glide,
  We're home at last, home at last;
  Softly we drift on its bright, silver tide,
  We're home at last, home at last.
  Glory to God! all our dangers are o'er,
  We stand secure on the glorified shore;
  Glory to God! we shall shout evermore;
  We're home at last, home at last.

THE FOUNTAIN OF LIFE.

232   The Fountain of Life.

1 All you that are weary and sad—come!
  And you that are cheerful and glad—
      come!
  In robes of humility clad—come!
  The Saviour invites you to-day.

2 Let youth in its freshness and bloom,
      come!
  Let man in the pride of his noon, come!
  Let age on the verge of the tomb, come!
  Let none in his pride stay away.

3 Let the halt, and the maimed, and the blind, come!
Let all who are freely inclined, come!
With an humble and peaceable mind, come!
Away from the waters of strife.

4 The Spirit and Bride freely say, Come!
And let him that heareth it say, Come!
And let him that thirsteth to-day, come!
And drink of the fountain of life.

THE EDEN ABOVE.

CHORUS.

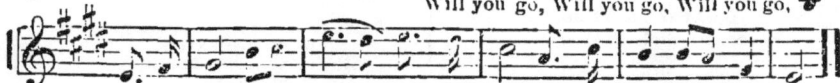

Will you go, Oh! say, Will you go to the E-den a-bove.

233 The Eden Above.

1 We're bound for the land of the pure and the holy,   [love,
The home of the happy, the kingdom of
Ye wanderers from God in the broad road of folly,
Oh, say, will you go to the Eden above?

2 In that blessed land neither sighing nor anguish   [lied rove;
Can breathe in the fields where the glori-
Ye heart-burden'd ones, who in misery languish,
Oh, say, will you go to the Eden above?

3 Nor fraud, nor deceit, nor the hand of oppression,   [grove;
Can injure the dwellers in that holy

No wickedness there, not a shade of transgression;
Oh, say, will you go to the Eden above?

4 No poverty there—no, the saints all are wealthy,   [love;
The heirs of His glory whose nature is
Nor sickness can reach them, that country is healthy;
Oh, say, will you go to the Eden above?

5 And yet, guilty sinner, we would not forsake thee,   [move;
We halt yet a moment as onward we
Oh, come to thy Lord, in his arms he will take thee,
And bear thee along to the Eden above.

WILL YOU GO?

FINE.

D. C.

234 Sinner's Invitation.

1 Will you go, sinner, go to the highlands of Heaven?
Where the storms never blow, and the long summer's given;
Where the bright, blooming flowers are their odors emitting,
And the leaves of the bowers, in the breezes are flitting.

2 Where the rich, golden fruit is in bright clusters pending,
And the deep-laden boughs of life's fair tree are bending,
And where life's crystal stream is unceasingly flowing,   [growing.
And the verdure is green, and eternally

3 Where the saints rob'd in white—cleans'd in life's flowing fountain,
Shining beauteous and bright, they inhabit the mountain;
Where no sin nor dismay, neither trouble nor sorrow,   [the morrow.
Will be felt for a day, nor be feared for

4 Look by faith to the cross, and behold Jesus bleeding,   [interceding,
Then, ascended on high, at the throne
Oh, secure pardon now, while sweet mercy's extended,   [is ended.
Ere the harvest is past and the summer

5 He's prepared thee a home—sinner, canst thou believe it?
And invites thee to come—sinner, wilt thou receive it?   [receding.
Oh, come, sinner, come, for the time is
And the Saviour will soon and forever cease pleading.

BETHANY. 6s & 4s.

235   Nearer to Thee.

1 Nearer, my God, to thee,
   Nearer to thee,
Ev'n though it be a cross
   That raiseth me,
Still all my song shall be,
Nearer, my God, to thee,
Nearer, my God, to thee,
   Nearer to thee.

2 Though like a wanderer,
   Daylight all gone,
Darkness be over me,
   My rest a stone;
Yet in my dreams I'd be
Nearer, my God, to thee,
Nearer, my God, to thee,
   Nearer to thee.

3 There let the way appear,
   Steps up to Heaven;
All that thou sendest me,
   In mercy given;
Angels to beckon me
Nearer, my God, to thee,
Nearer, my God, to thee,
   Nearer to thee.

4 Then, with my waking thoughts
   Bright with thy praise,
Out of my stony griefs
   Bethel I'll raise;
So by my woes to be
Nearer, my God, to thee,
Nearer, my God, to thee,
   Nearer to thee.

SWEET HOUR OF PRAYER. L. M. Double.

236   Sweet Hour of Prayer.

1 Sweet hour of prayer! sweet hour of
   prayer!
That calls me from a world of care,
And bids me, at my Father's throne,
Make all my wants and wishes known.
In seasons of distress and grief,
My soul has often found relief,
And oft escaped the tempter's snare
By thy return, sweet hour of prayer.

2 Sweet hour of prayer! sweet hour of
   prayer!
Thy wings shall my petition bear
To Him whose truth and faithfulness

Engage the waiting soul to bless.
And since he bids me seek his face,
Believe his word, and trust his grace,
I'll cast on him my every care,
And wait for thee, sweet hour of prayer.

3 Sweet hour of prayer! sweet hour of
   prayer!
May I thy consolation share,
Till from Mount Pisgah's lofty height,
I view my home and take my flight.
In my immortal flesh I'll rise
To seize the everlasting prize,
And shout, while passing thro' the air,
Farewell, farewell, sweet hour of prayer.

INDEX.

Titles in Small Caps.—First Lines in Roman.

INDEX OF SUBJECTS.

METRICAL INDEX.

www.ingramcontent.com/pod-product-compliance
Lightning Source LLC
Chambersburg PA
CBHW030538270326
41927CB00008B/1431